C000181794

THE VANISHING RELICS
OF BARNSLEY

THE VANISHING RELICS OF BARNSLEY

by Gerald J. Alliott

Wharncliffe Publishing Limited

**First published in 1996 by
Wharncliffe Publishing Limited**

Copyright © Gerald Alliott

*For up-to-date information on other titles produced
under the Wharncliffe imprint, please telephone or
write to:*
Wharncliffe Publishing Limited
FREEPOST
47 Church Street,
Barnsley,
South Yorkshire S70 2BR
Telephone (24 hours): 01226 734555

ISBN: 1 871647 29 0

*All rights reserved. No part of this publication may be reproduced,
stored in a retrieval system, or transmitted, in any form or by any
means, electronic, mechanical, photocopying, recording or otherwise,
without prior permission in writing of the publishers.*
*This book is sold subject to the condition that it shall not, by way of
trade or otherwise, be lent, resold, hired out or otherwise circulated
without the publisher's prior consent in any form of binding or cover
other than that in which it is published and without a similiar
condition including this condition being imposed on the subsequent
purchaser.*

A CIP catalogue record of this book is available from the British
Library

Printed in Great Britain by
Redwood Books Limited, Trowbridge, Wiltshire

CONTENTS

FOREWORD

'Fortiter occupa portam...'

Surviving fellow alumni of that fine old relic of Barnsley, the Archbishop Holgate Grammar School of the 1930s, will probably remember the above opening line of the school song which translated freely as 'Ever be bold, the gate to hold'. In 1938, as a boy of 11 years, albeit enjoying a first year of classical education under the great custodian of those halls of academe, Dr. Schooling, I had many years to go before I would really know anything at all about holding gates, particularly those wonderful portals opening to the past and its memories. In his *Vanishing Relics of Barnsley*, my brother, Gerald, has opened, and gone through, such a gate with all of the determination and verve of the true historian giving us a fascinating montage, and invoking many treasured memories, of what was a fine old Yorkshire town before it became entangled in the tentacles of the haphazard, commercially-greedy, memory-erasing and inevitable monster of urban renewal.

I was born in 1927 at a house on Barnsley Road in the village of Cudworth. The days of the steam train were at their height and the old 'push-and-pull' puffed along on its frequent daily runs to Barnsley and back. Our grandfather was the Foreman at Cudworth station, the largest open-air station in the country - now another vanished relic. My formative years, from around the age of 6 years almost to the time of the commencement of the Second World War, were spent with my brother and sister at my father's pub, the Hope Inn, on the bank of the old Barnsley canal, long since filled in. In retrospect, it seems to me that Gerald and I enjoyed many halcyon days of discovery and exploration in and around the town. Our daily walks to school from Cundy Cross to town, and back, were expeditions never exceeded, in their sense of adventure, by many of those journeys of the great explorers of our history books. The great journeys of Scott and Amundsen, Stanley and Livingstone, and their like, could not compare with those of our youth when life was so new and vital. Beevor Bridge at Hoyle Mill was a lingering point where we would savour the malty smell from the brewery and prepare ourselves for the heat and noise whilst passing the glassworks. Most days we would be late home from school much to the despair of our harassed mother with yet another 'spoilt' tea on her hands. Incurring the wrath of an irate parent was a small price to pay after yet another 'Everest' had been climbed - and, surely, it must be that those early days of great adventure partly formed the shell from which one day a local historian would emerge.

I am very honoured and pleased that my brother has asked me to write a few words as a foreword to his book. Unlike me, he did not desert his home town in his adult years. His love for his town, and his desire for the preservation of what remains of his heritage as a Barnsley man, is very evident throughout the book. On my first browsing through its pages I felt lost memories flowing back like the hidden waters of the Sough, and that is what a book of this nature is all about - but it goes beyond nostalgia. It is a dedication to our forebears and to their design and craftsmanship, and to the honesty and integrity of their work. The 18th. century poet and writer, William Cowper, wrote, 'God made the country, and man made the town'. How sad to discover that, in many instances, the wonderful old towns of his day have been plundered and sacked by the robber barons of modern commerce, leaving on the sites of their waste land our red brick enclaves of cheap emporia together with the glass and chrome of the towering office temples.

In wandering down memory lane, one is often reminded of the old adage that it is easier to pull down than to build. Fortunately, there are people around who record momentous events and worthy places. There are also people, like my brother, who research the records in an effort to preserve the past, if only in memory. His book has given me great pleasure as it will to many other Barnsley men and women.

Ernest E. Alliott
Chairman of International Preparatory Schools Limited
Singapore

INTRODUCTION

'The past will not sleep, it works still, with every new fact a ray of light shoots up from the long buried years.'

Ralph Waldo Emerson

Some time ago I was handed a map showing Barnsley in 1777 at the time of the Enclosure Award, but what really interested me was a feint pencil note at the foot of the map, 'Catholic school bell was on the Moot Hall'. On reading this note my first thoughts were 'for whom the bell tolled'. My interest in this inspired me to write *The Vanishing Relics of Barnsley*, not as a difinitive work but for the interest and pleasure of those who love the past.

The Sough Dyke known by many of Barnsley's older inhabitants as 'The water behind the Ritz', is one of our oldest links with former years so this is where I shall begin my story.

I hope my readers will not be content by just reading this book, but put on a strong pair of boots and enjoy, too, the pleasure I had in seeking out these remains of our past, most of which I discovered by the process of reasoning, observation and deduction - not imagination or fantasy - together with the help of many whom I have mentioned in my list of acknowledgements.

In writing this I make no apologies and no pretence of being anything but another enthusiastic amateur historian. It has been a labour of love and the research and discovery has given me infinite gratification.

G.J. Alliott
Barnsley, 1996

Part One

THE RIVER SOUGH AND ITS TRIBUTARIES
OR 'A RIVULET CALLED TUNBROOK'

About the year 1280 Alexander Portbref granted, by deed, to Thomas, son of Robert del Rodis, a messuage in the town of Barnsley near the way called Westgate, towards the Rivulet called 'Tunbrook'.

Although this is the earliest unmistakable reference to the Sough that I have found, it has been stated, but I feel this to be partly supposition, that the Romans probably formed the embankments of the Sough and the Dearne, since the Saxons, named the one 'Sough Dyke' and the other t'old Dyke, however it has certainly always been one of the main arteries of Barnsley, which is itself an important crossroads of the North. It was also referred to in 1633, in an old account book, by its present name 'Sough Dike' when a Widow Hinchliffe was said to have lived nearby and received charity.

Much has been written in the past, on this subject, by eminent local historians, but I found something exciting about exploring the springs, tributaries and course of this almost forgotten part of our history, from its source at Whinney Nook to where it ends its journey at Hoyle Mill and joins the Dearne.

I hope my experience will be of interest and encourage future students of our local history to follow the now sighing water of the Sough.

In early days the River Sough, now known as the Sough Dyke, had quite a prolific flow, from which it gained its name, and together with numerous springs and wells, was the main source of our domestic water supply - I wonder if we now appreciate the true value of the humble tap?

The Sough is now only a trickle except when it shows its true self in stormy weather. Its decline, together with many rivers which were once raging currents, increased as the Industrial Revolution, with its many new mills, became increasingly thirsty and demanding. History is once more repeating itself, with our present water supply, at times, undergoing changes in a similar manner; many rivers, especially in the South, are drying up.

Until the early part of the 19th century the water in the Sough was clean and pure and contained fish and wildlife. Later when it reached the new mills and dye-houses of the linen industry and functioned as the main drain for the town, it was uncovered and passed down the main street. Visitors were not impressed.

Let us now commence our journey at the place known as Whinney

Barnsley c1820

The place known as Whinney Nook, Dodworth Road.

Nook, a place situated between Pogmoor and Dodworth Road and the site of the spring-head. But is it? Rowland Jackson, one of our leading historians, in 1858 said, 'the Sough rises at Whinney Nook' but another unknown person had other views and said 'this is hardly correct, there may be one source there but the original source is higher up within a short distance of Keresforth Hill; it then flows almost due north under Broadway via Beaumont Avenue, under Dodworth Road by S.R. Gent & Co. and in a north easterly direction, finally joining the Sough at Whinney Nook.' The reader must judge for himself, but I feel that Jackson was correct and that the stream from Keresforth is one of a number of tributaries which I will describe as we continue the journey.

The Dyke was sometimes known as Whinney Nook Dyke as far as Summer Lane and then Sough Dyke but I will refer to it all as the Sough.

To get our first glimpse of this elusive waterway we follow the railway line behind the Polar Garage to the bottom of May Terrace where it can just be seen below the grassy bank. Not much there, although it is dry weather at the moment, so we will continue further down Dodworth Road and walk to the rear of Springfield Street (no doubt where it got its name from), where the old Barnsley British Co-operative Society Corn Mill was built in 1880. The Mill reservoir, which was fed by the Sough, supplied the Lancashire Boilers which raised the steam for the 400 horse-power horizontal engine used to drive the plant in the Mill.

Although an untidy mess and partly concealed by rubbish and

The culvert behind Springfield Street.

undergrowth, the brick arched culvert that conveys the water, once more underground, can be seen. It then flows under Farrar Street down to Summer Lane where it once supplied the reservoir of the old Iron Foundry which was built in the 1820s by Messrs Woodiwiss & Faulds. Across Summer Lane the steep incline towards Sackville Street turned the Sough towards Townend where the Calender Pond and Pumps once stood, an area where many floods have been experienced, some deep enough for boating and swimming. The Calender Pond depended upon the Sough for a good supply of water, it was well walled round in stone and the water was quite pure in the early 1800s, when John Burland, another local historian, remembered seeing goldfish swimming in it. Positioned at the front of the Pond were two pumps which supplied the local domestic needs, one had a short arm for normal use and one a longer arm for filling water barrels. There was also a trough for the animals. Nearby were the Union and Hope Calender Mills, in fact there were no less than five Mills in this area, each having its own reservoir fed by the Sough.

The Calender was romantically portrayed in Robert McLintock's poem in 1839:

THE UNION CALENDER.

Behold its beauty, and likewise its strength,
With its dimensions, both its width and length:
Observe its ponderous walls, and massive doors,
With its majestic roof, and solid floors.
And pools of water doth likewise abound, -
Floating on the surface, and below the ground.
Likewise, observe, how well this place is fenced,
With stones well-hewn, and well-cemented.
But now, advance into its inward parts,
And see the beauty of sublimer arts.
Behold its power, from whence did it derive it:
Or how, did feeble man at first contrive it?
I know the cause - the same I'll not conceal.
It first proceeded from the smitten steel.
One spark proceeding ushered into flame,
And soon a mighty furnace it became;
The flame dissolves the water, makes it swell,
And then the boiler does completely fill:
The active liquid foaming and expanding,
Forcing the wheels, impelling and commanding.
But there are many causes and conductors.
Which help the motion, and become supporters:
And when the water is combined with fire,

The massive stones move forward and retire.
When these two elements, called fire and water.
Co-operate together in this matter:
When they in contact come, their powers they play,
And on the wheels they give an awful sway.
By this easy, simple, powerful plan,
Iron, wood, and stone do labour hard for man.
When this strong engine doth its work perform,
Then it resembles a great thunder-storm.
Thus waring elements produce thunder,
Moving the hills, and tearing rocks asunder.
Oh that my feeble mind could now expand!
Then secret causes I would understand,
Then I would soar among the starry train;
Then I would dive into the wat'ry main:
Then I would know how the moon doth guide -
The foaming billows and the swelling tide.
Then I would know, tho' I am low in station,
The mighty wonders that are in creation.

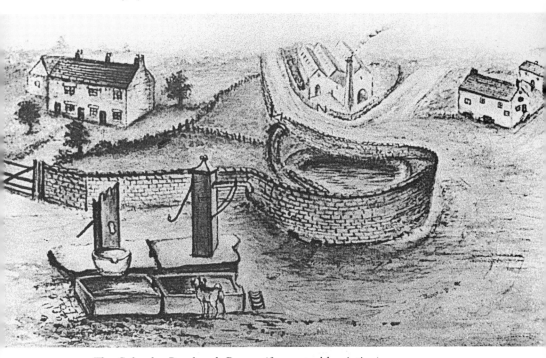

The Calender Pond and Pumps (from an old painting).

Opposite the Calender pond at the bottom of Shambles Street (formerly Westgate) stood a beerhouse, later known to us as Townend Chemist, demolished only a few years ago. It was opened in 1829 by Tom Toppin under the sign of 'Water Joe' and on the sign was a representation of old Joe with his water barrel.

Water Joe was born Joseph Broadhead in Nottingham in 1772 but came to Barnsley and lived for a time by the Windmill near to Churchfields. He was a born wit, joking with all he met and became one of our well known local characters of the day. He was selling water in 1811 when the local population was only 5014 but by 1821 it had increased to 8284 living in

1441 houses and was totally dependent on water from wells, springs and the Sough, consequently business for Joe was very good. He continued selling water from his cart until 1842 but business was now declining due to the advent of the passing of the Barnsley Waterworks Act in 1837, allowing water to be drawn from the Dearne and eventually piped to all the houses and works in the Town. Old Joe died in 1852, aged 80 years, at his small apartment near Beckett Square, for which he paid rent of 9d per week.

On the other side of Townend stood the old Post Office, a building similar and about the same age as Water Joe's, with a decorative carved wood facade and round arched windows. This too was recently demolished to make way for the new relief road, however, it is pleasing to know that part of it was saved at the last minute, from the bulldozers, by

Water Joe in 1841.   our local Historic Buildings Officer, John Hislop, and is now stored, perhaps one day to be rebuilt and shown as a representative part of Barnsley in the 19th century.

The two buildings had lots of things in common but, nothing moreso than the heavy flooding they both suffered when the Sough was under pressure during rain storms.

At Townend the Sough received water from the old Shaw Well, on Shaw Lane, via Grafton Street and under the now demolished Wheatsheaf Hotel at the bottom of Racecommon Road. It no doubt supplied the Oak Linen Mill on its way down. Another tributary flowed from the rear of the Fire Station on Broadway and joined the water from the Shaw Well at a site on Shaw Lane on which once stood the reservoir of the old Shaw Mill.

There were two pumps over the Shaw well, similar to the ones at Townend, little and large. The well yielded a copious supply of water for

Townend c1880. Old buildings and site of the Calender Pond on the left.

The Shaw Well and Pumps this century and no longer in use.

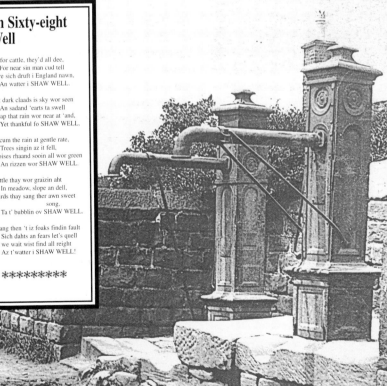

Eighteen Hundred an Sixty-eight An Shaw Well

T'YEAR sixty-eight ah can't forget,
   Nor yit omit to tell!
The wunders ov that marvellous year,
   An that too ov SHAW WELL.

Week after week, munth after munth,
   No rain or dew ere fell,
An poands an pumps no watter had,
   Yet plenty had SHAW WELL.

Thus t'glass wor tapt full oft ta see,
   What t'finger sure wod tell,
But at 'Set Fair' it ivver wor,
   Yet runnin wor SHAW WELL.

Nah far and near, an near an far,
   For self an for ta sell,
Did barrils cum, day after day
   Ta fill at this SHAW WELL.

Disheartend nah wor timid foaks,
   An went soar far ta tell
At thear na rain wod fall all t'year,
   An dry wod be SHAW WELL.

An more than that, they'd ruined be,
   For nowt they'd hev ta sell,
Az corn an hay wod be burnt up,
   An dry wod be SHAW WELL.

An az for cattle, they'd all dee,
   For near sin man cud tell
Wor ere sich druft i England nawn,
   An watter i SHAW WELL.

At last dark claads is sky wor seen
   An sadand 'earts ta swell
We hoap that rain wor near at 'and,
   Yet thankful fo SHAW WELL.

Dahn cum the rain at gentle rate,
   Trees singin az it fell,
An cloises rhaand sooin all wor green
   An rizzen wor SHAW WELL.

An cattle thay wor graizin aht
   In meadow, slope an dell,
An burds thay sang ther awn sweet
                                    song,
   Ta t' bubblin ov SHAW WELL.

Hah rang then 't iz foaks findin fault
   Sich dahts an fears let's quell
For if we wait wist find all reight
   Az t'watter i SHAW WELL!

****

the local inhabitants which was pure and was collected in large water barrels, pulled by horses, to be sold all over town by characters like Water Joe. The underground reservoir behind the pumps is quite large, about 40 feet by 20 feet and although we know it is about 17 feet deep, stories were once told, in order to keep children away, as to the unfathomable depth of the well. The question was answered in 1826 when the water dried up for the first time. Perhaps you will be amused by the poem, written in our own language, to commemorate the unusual event.

Little is now left at the site of the pumps except the stone walls of the enclosure and the underground reservoir with its usual level of water, to remind us of another vanished relic of the past.

Back at Townend, the site of the Calender Pond was donated, on 1 October, 1901, to the Mayor, Aldermen and Burgesses of the Borough of Barnsley by the Rev Thomas Thornely Taylor, in memory of his father, Thomas Edward Taylor JP, 'to be preserved for ever for the free use and enjoyment of the public'. The site was filled in and a park created. A plaque was erected which has now been removed to Cannon Hall for safe custody from the vandals.

The Sough now crossed over to what, at the time of the Enclosure, was a deep valley covered in vegetation and bracken. On one side it rose steeply towards Westgate and Pinfold Hill and on the south side, up towards Peasehills or what we now know as Pitt Street. Part of the area was, at one time, an ancient enclosure known as 'The Tumbling Hills': this must surely try one's imagination to the full.

During the 1820s, Charles Tee, a linen manufacturer, of Pindar Oaks, purchased land in this area together with watercourses. In 1828 on this site, the firm of Richardson, Tee & Rycroft opened the Bore Spring Linen Mill, later the site of the Ritz cinema where many local people will remember crossing a wooden bridge over the water to the car park. A reservoir and sluice were formed by the Sough and by 1840 powered looms were in use. In 1851 the firm produced a magnificent table cloth in fine damask. The dimensions of it were 307 feet x 8 feet, it weighed 2 cwts and cost £50 for a Mr M Soyer of London. The reservoir was joined here by another tributary which flowed from High Stile Field (now Locke Park) down to Porter's High Stile and Longcar Pits, then down Racecommon and on under York Street to join the Sough at the Bore Spring Mill.

As we move along what is now Peel Street but keeping in mind what it must have been like long ago, the next point of interest and importance is the last remaining section of the old Sough bed, as it was, when it flowed uncovered through the Town. It can be seen behind the now disused filling station, next to the King George Hotel (Kingsleys) or from the car park of Leo's supermarket. This section dried up when in 1974/75 the Sough was

The old Sough bed, off Peel Street, now overgrown.

diverted, as part of a flood relief scheme, through a large concrete sewer from Townend, down Peel Street, to Peel Square where it rejoined the old stone culvert and back on its original course.

Whilst not wishing to sound too cynical, I can imagine developers rapidly disposing of this interesting part of our industrial history. Most of the filling station site itself was occupied by quite a large reservoir, fed by the Sough, which supplied the steam engine in the corn mill next door. Part

The Mill after 1910.

The Mill building, 1992.

of the mill site is now taken up by the Hotel but the interesting thing is a section of the original mill next door still standing after nearly 200 years and now used as a retail store.

The mill was actually built in 1821 on part of the area known as 'Peasehills' and 'The Tumbling Hills'. It was complete with steam engine, 5 pairs of grinding stones, hoppers and boilers and early in 1822 it was sold to Thomas Rycroft, common carrier. It continued as a mill until early this century, after which it was purchased in 1910 by George Booker, proprietor of the Millstone Inn next door and, used as a garage.

From the mill reservoir, the Sough flowed under the mill buildings and crossed to the other side of the valley. At that time there was no road past the mill towards Dodworth; Peel Street was laid down much later. By 1837, after the new Waterworks Act was passed, and not forgetting the Coronation, many new streets were opened; the population had increased to about 15,000 and 4,000 handlooms were now in operation within the town, with a turnover of about £1,000,000. The Sough having crossed what was known as Steam Mill Lane, crossed the bottom of Dog Lane, an ancient footpath, adjacent to Thomas Summers' Ropewalk. The footpath traversed the Sough and continued onto Barnsley Common where it separated, going in two directions. This part of the Sough in earlier days was occupied by fish, much to the delight of the boys from Westgate who spent many happy hours with rod and line and, perhaps, a bent pin with worm.

Nearby, in 1845, Thomas Taylor's Linen Mill was established and became one of the largest in the area, eventually to have as many as 430 powered looms and one of the last in Barnsley to close its doors, due to cheap foreign imports.

From Dog Lane the Sough flowed along the north side of the valley towards Peel Square then under the old pack-horse bridge at the bottom of Market Hill, opposite what was the Coach & Horses Hotel, now a bank. Before Peel Street was opened, Peel Square was divided by a row of old shops and a Bakehouse, occupied by Henry Machen. The south side was known as Peasehills Nook and the north side as Sough Bridge. These old buildings were purchased, in 1839, by the Town Commissioners and

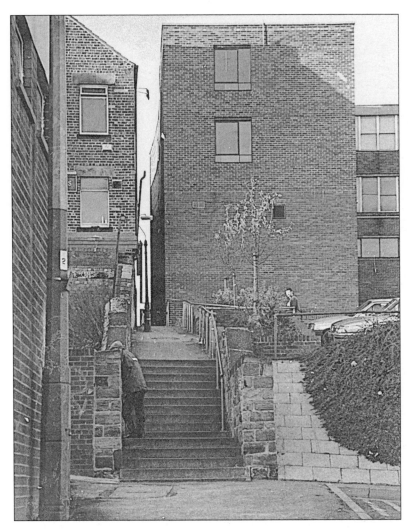

Useful thoroughfare known as Dog Lane, 1995.

demolished to make a better way for the new road to Townend.

Here I will endeavour to settle a controversy as to the flow of the Sough between the Corn Mill and Sough Bridge. It has been argued that when the water flowed from the Mill, it continued along the south side and came through a passage at the rear of the old Chronicle Buildings and across Peel Square. I am quite sure that this was never the case; the passage was actually a back entrance to the Freeman's Arms on Peel Street, and was also almost identical to a similar passage leading to the old Lord Nelson, in Mitchell's yard on Queen Street. The original course is shown on 18th century maps and never changed until 1974/75 when the flood relief scheme was implemented, as previously mentioned. The only water supply near this old passage was an old well which, at one time, fed a pump by the doorway of the shoe shop, next to the Chronicle Buildings. When Robinson & Son were digging the foundations, in 1876, for the new Chronicle Building the well was uncovered and found to still have a good supply of water.

In 1993 when the Old Chronicle Building was being converted to a public house, 'Tommy Wallocks', I was asked to inspect a spring which had been uncovered in the basement. I concluded that it was, without doubt, the original spring which, at one time, fed a pump behind the old shop next door. The water was still clear and fresh. The last time it had been seen was in 1876 when Robinson & Sons came across it during the construction of the foundations.

Hoping that I have put the record straight, let us now look at one of the most interesting sections of the Sough, which was at a lower level than at the present time. We know that parts of the early packhorse bridge, which was later replaced by a wooden one, still exist together with the old stone culvert and arches below the road at the bottom of Market Hill. If any reader has any photographs of this area, taken in 1974/75, when it was all uncovered, I would be most interested to see them. This part, then known as Sough Bridge, was renamed Queen Street in 1837, when Queen Victoria came to the throne, although the old name was remembered many years later in a deed as late as 1884, which describes Joseph Mitchell's property at the end of Market Street as being near a place formerly called Sough Bridge but now called Peel Square.

The bridge was narrow with side walls, on which it was said, the idlers and gossip mongers, probably joined by Martha Clarke, landlady of the Cross Daggers Inn, would swap their tales. At one side of the bridge there were stepping stones for the use of pedestrians.

A very sad accident happened at the bottom of Market Hill in October 1831. A hawker woman named Burrows, aged nearly 90, was crossing the bridge with her barrow when the five o'clock 'Red Rover' coach, from the King's Head to Sheffield, hit her. She was dreadfully mangled and had to have one arm amputated on the spot, but unfortunately she died a few days later and an inquest was held on Monday, 7 November, 1831, at the Lord Nelson, when Thomas Hawkesworth was the landlord. The verdict was accidental death and a deodand was awarded for £7-10s against the coach and horses. Before 1846 a deodand was a legal award granted against the object which caused damage or injury.

Another well documented incident was, of course, when Sam Truelove,

Peel Square (Peasehills Nook) early this century.

whose Smithy was opposite the Sough Bridge at the bottom of the Hill, shot and killed John Fish, a rag gatherer of Hoylandswaine. It was in June 1787 when the old Smithy and other old buildings were in pretty bad shape and ready for demolition, much to the dismay of Sam (they must have had compulsory purchase orders even in those days) who climbed up onto his roof with his gun. Fish then boldly climbed aloft and started pulling the slates off the building which was too much for Sam who, after two attempts, finally shot and killed him. He was apprehended and tried at York, represented by local Solicitors, Richard Fenton and Jonas Clarke who petitioned the jury to return a verdict of manslaughter. He was fined £20 and went to prison for two years, eventually being discharged in a very poor state of health when it was said that his toes had rotted off. He died within a few years, is interred in St. Mary's churchyard and perhaps should have taken note of his neighbour, Tommy Morton, a Tinker, who kept a bear to protect his property! however, that, too, was demolished. On a lighter note Charles Rogers (Tom Treddlehoyle) wrote of the famous

Bill for repairs to the Town Pump

football matches on Market Hill, in his usual vernacular manner:-
  "Full menny a fooit-ball match on't Markit-hill,
  That's nah neer seen, nor happan nivver will;
  An oft wor seen, az boath sides feircely play'd,
  Sum two or three it sough-dyke sprawlin laid."
Just below Sam Truelove's Smithy and above the Sough was the Town
Pump and well, it had a hood over it and supplied water for the town centre
and market area. When the old buildings were pulled down the road was
raised and the well covered over. Steps were built down to it but the
animals could no longer reach it. An interesting account from 1745, for

repairs to the Town Pump by Robert Robinson is shown opposite.

The pump was eventually done away with in the 1820's because it interfered with wagons belonging to Mr Ridsdale, Carrier and Landlord of the White Hart, making a sharp turn into the Hotel yard. Mr Ridsdale must have had influence and importance for the Town Commissioners to have allowed this Capital pump to be removed as early as that time.

The Sough now continued, through a culvert, along, what is now Eldon Street, but in earlier times this area was mainly gardens owned by families and local property owners like the Kendrays who Kendray Street was named after. It passed the old Three Cranes Hotel, crossing the top of the Burlington Arcade where a large manhole had been constructed at the beginning of this century in which they deposited snow during bad winters - an event which I remember from the 1940s and 50s. The Sough then crossed Kendray Street and continued across Jumble Lane to what was Beckett Square where it was traversed by a rustic bridge behind the Gas Works and later arched over. At this point it was joined by a tributary known as Barker Brook which was of paramount importance to the inhabitants, mostly weavers, of an area known as Wilson's Piece, named after William Wilson, the founder of our linen industry. It supplied this area with all of its domestic water until well after the 1837 Waterworks Act and in the 18th century it had quite a gushing flow through a wild common but its course was, like the Sough itself, subject to controversy. It was described by John Burland as having its source in a field near a footpath leading from Dawson's Wall (New Street) to Racecommon flowing in an almost straight line down and parallel to the north side of Dawson's Wall, crossing the south side of May Day Green and joining the Sough at the north-east corner of the Gas Works. He also describes a further tributary running a little north of Barker Brook to the south end of Nelson Street foundry, through Wellington Street, across the old Royal Oak Croft (near to the present Corner Pin) and then on to May Day Green, either joining Barker Brook or direct into the Sough. He also mentioned Peasehills Pond between the two foundries, which was formed by blocking up this second tributary although most maps since 1850, including Ordnance Survey and more modern drainage maps show only one tributary, (Barker Brook) flowing from its previously described source but direct to the foundry pond and not down Dawson's Wall. My own opinion is that Barker Brook did, originally, flow down New Street, then via May Day Green to join the Sough. In the 18th centur, at the bottom of New Street, stood a small group of houses, one being Bark House near Barker Bridge, named after Barker Brook. In 1865 Thomas Summers, rope manufacturer, as a devisee of Abraham and Thomas Ely deceased, sold a messuage or dwellinghouse and shop in Newlands (New Street) near Barker Bridge, formerly used as a Public House. There are various other references to New Street in the 18th century as being a quiet country lane, wooded on either side with a stream running its entire length, its source being in Far Well Field and joining the Sough Dyke near Beckett Square. It is possible that a diversion was created from Barker Brook in the Agnes Road area leading direct to the foundries and Peasehills Pond, this being mistaken for the second tributary. However, perhaps somebody will oppose my opinion and I will certainly leave it open to refutation.

Before leaving this region another sad day is brought to mind when recalling Whit Tuesday, 12 June, 1832, when a dreadful storm occurred causing a waterspout to burst over the upper reaches of the Sough valley. The Dyke turned into a furious river and was waist high by the time it reached Queen Street. Much damage was done, pigs drowned in their sties, cellars filled up, May Day Green was a lake and tradesmen lost heavily, especially the grocers. Even hedgehogs and rats were borne along with the tide but this did not discourage one local character, Jack Stanton, from removing his clothes to swim in the street. Dr Sadler, the Medical Officer of Health, reported, in his annual report, that the flood had helped to propogate cholera, particularly in areas populated mainly by manual labour like Wilson's Piece. The outbreak had originally started in India in 1831 and passed to England early in 1832 claiming a total of 295 people during that year, including Dr Dow on 9 October, due to his devotion to the cholera patients.

The Sough, on leaving the Gas Works and having received all its major tributaries, headed towards the Mount Osbourne Colliery which was sunk in 1837 by Richard Day of Monk Bretton on farm land owned by the Duke of Leeds, near the present Pontefract Road.

Here at Mount Osbourne, I have once more to relate, of disaster and great sadness. On Sunday, 15 July, 1883, at about half past one an alarming thunderstorm broke over the town, accompanied by rain, hail and lightning. The Sough passed under the road to the Colliery yard through a large culvert; a number of children were playing nearby and rushed into the culvert to shelter from the storm, not realizing that all the water from the town would shortly pass through it. They were not in it very long before this happened and all of them were rushed off their feet and carried along with the water. After leaving the Colliery road the Dyke was once more open and three of them managed, with great difficulty, to climb out but the rest, being five in number, were swept along down the valley, partly through another culvert under Beevor Hall. Three bodies were found, after a long search and another one the following day, but it was Tuesday before the last body, a young girl, Ada Chambers, was finally located, in the Dearne. The verdict of the Coroner's jury was 'accidentally drowned'.

Johnnie Scott in Beevor Hole.

There were many other storms of note in Barnsley, in 1856, 1860/61, 11 June and 18 July, 1872 and during a really bad one on 15 August, 1791, it was reported that a girl was struck blind.

About 1840, near the Mount Osbourne Colliery and not far from the Oakwell, workmen were digging and found the remains of an old mill whose stonework and watercourse were in fine condition as were millstones and even part of the waterwheel. The mill probably dated from the times of the Monks of Pontefract and could have been the original soke mill, but it was certainly driven by the waters of the Sough when it was more of a river than a dyke.

Here, and not being too familiar with Beevor Hole or Hoyle, I recruited the help of Johnnie Scott of Barugh Green, a man with 30 years' knowledge of the Sough and the local drains, although now retired. We climbed down into the valley behind Oakwell football ground with the sun shining through the trees and my mind went back to the time before the Enclosure when it was described as 'a charming rural dell through which the Barnsley rivulet, anciently known as the River Sough, in playful eddies

Beevor Hall shortly before its demolishion.

and rippling gushes, sauntered merrily along to the bosom of the umbrageous Dearne'. The water in those days was plentiful and full of fish, being also a favourite home of water hens and wildlife.

It was at that time a romantic valley with a footpath running along the east side of the river, looking up towards the Queen's Grounds. The west side was a steep incline up to Bunkers Hill, which was named the Whin Bank, in recognition of a thick covering of furze which, in the Spring, turned yellow making a very cheerful sight. At the foot of the Whin Bank bubbled the Oakwell, a clear soft spring of sweet water, good for bleaching and preserving the colour of linen. An interesting local custom was the Household linen being washed at the well and dried on the Whin Bank, by the servant girls. While the linen was drying, bottles of home brewed ale were opened and food spread on the grass to make a picnic when the girls would often be joined by their sweet-hearts to enjoy the occasion.

The valley became famous for linen bleaching and in the 18th century, William Wilson, previously mentioned as the founder of our linen industry, brought bleachers across the Pennines and established bleach works there and at other places in the locality.

About 1813, William Jackson (linen) purchased land at Beevor Hole, built the Hall and with James Lister carried on an extensive linen business for about 25 years. In 1833 he walled off the Oakwell, as it was on his land, but he piped the water, through lead pipes to the bleach croft. However this did not go down very well with the water carriers who cut the pipes in order to conserve their living.

By 1850, due to the dye houses, mills and drains, the Sough, on its final stretch, and now called the Sough Dyke, became a fetid sewer in which nothing, even tadpoles could survive. In 1855 the Medical Officer of Health having inspected it declared it to be injurious to the health of the local inhabitants and as the area became more polluted the bleach crofts gradually moved away to cleaner places out of the town.

In more recent times, the Sough, at Beevor Hole, has seen beer, bobbins and glass, but once more the valley is quiet and, although it is difficult to get through the undergrowth, the atmosphere is still very appealing. At one time I imagined I could hear whispers from the past, but perhaps it was just the gentle sigh of the waters, after centuries, still wending their way, now underground, through a large brick culvert, on a final journey. Behind the old chapel at Hoyle Mill, it is joined by the Measbrough Dyke and then through a large concrete outlet to its final confluence with the River Dearne.

The Sough ends its journey as it joins the Dearne.

Part Two

THE MOOTHALL RELICS
'Sad relics of departed worth' - Byron

Before I recount the history and travels of the relics, perhaps a few words about the Moot Hall (town hall) itself, although it has been well described and portrayed by numerous historians in the past.

The building, erected about 1680, stood at the head of Market Hill and was on the site of an earlier Hall. It was mentioned in a curious undated document, but thought to be c.1676, addressed to His Majesty's Justices of the Peace for the West Riding of Yorkshire and signed by a number of prominent citizens of the town, certifying that "wee have erected a very convenient sessions hall in our said towne, therefore desire that the Quarter Sessions for the said Rydeins may be kept at our said towne as formerly'. Two of the signatories to the document died in the years 1683 and 1684 so it is quite possible that the presumed date of the document was not far wrong.

In referring to the earlier structure, of unknown provenance, the building, in 1611, must have been in a very poor condition when Francis Everingham (last of the Stainborough family) wrote to the Lord Treasurer, the Earl of Salisbury, complaining that the court house (Moot Hall) in Barnsley required speedy repairs. In 1622 in the town accounts an item appears as:-

Payde for they Moulthall dore keaye and ye locke
mendings to John Roolin . . . . viijd

Edmund Rogers (Collector of the Queen's rents for Barnsley), left, by his will dated 11 January, 1646, a bequest of ten pounds towards procuring a clock for the Moot Hall.

In 1660 it appears from Keresforth's deed relating to the establishment of a Grammar School, that there was an annual rent charged upon the shops below the Moot Hall, towards the support of the schoolmaster.

The Hall consisted of a large Justice Room, built in stone, above a row of small shops and was reached by a flight of 30 steps at the north-east corner; a large double window at the north end and three windows at both sides provided light. It has been said that Quarter Sessions were held here as far back as Edward III when they were first instituted, but it has also been said that they went back to the time of James I. We cannot be sure of the exact time of their inauguration, but we do know that on 14 October, 1794, Francis Edmunds of Worsbrough was Chairman of the last Sessions held in the old Moot Hall, which by now was in a very dilapidated state.

An artist's reconstruction based upon the description given.

Below the north end of the Hall, the building was colonnaded, using a traditional brick design in contrast to the stonework above and on market days this part was used for the sale of butter, poultry and eggs and on other days it was used by William Crossland, the stall setter, who lived next door to store the market stalls. In one of the cellars below the shops was the gaol, known as the 'Grate' which had a heavy oak door with iron studs

Market Hill in 1785 (from Lodges's Almanack*) The Moot Hall was above the row of shops.*

opposite the Minerva Printing Office, just below where Elstone's shop was later situated.

In 1750 a Bookseller named Joseph Smith was the occupier of one of the shops and later Thomas Cockshutt, by marrying Smith's daughter, succeeded to the business to become one of the last residents before the building was demolished.

On the west side of the Hall, by the market, stood a pillory and below

Barnsley Market Place - 100 years later - c.1885/90.

this were the town stocks, however, I will say more on this subject later.

On 15 May, 1822, an Act of Parliament was passed for 'Lighting, Paving, Cleansing, Watching and Improving the Town of Barnsley in the West Riding of Yorkshire'. A Board of 69 Commissioners was appointed to execute this Act, over an area of 1200 yards from all ways from the site of the late Moot Hall.

At one of the first meetings, held on 11 June, 1822, an order was made to purchase the site of the Moot Hall (now vacant) together with other properties on the market place. The Hall had been demolished about 1820 but the materials, together with materials from other nearby buildings, were sold by public auction on 14 August, 1823, the Auctioneer being Mr William Lancaster, also Landlord of the Talbot Inn. The sale in twelve lots, realized a total of £155-3s and it was stipulated that the materials should be cleared and carried away between 14 September and 10 October (later changed to 16 October). The vacant site was purchased, after delays and argument, for the sum of £350, from Joseph and John Clarke and John Hopwood, the devisees of James Carr; it was then added to the market area. In December 1829 the Commissioners ordered that Market Hill should now be paved during the course of which the architect in charge, Mr John Whitworth, marked the west and south boundaries of the Moot Hall with setts laid the opposite way. Unfortunately, these markings were abandoned in later years, due to the ignorance of the Authorities of that time.

The Moot Hall Plaque

A very important and exciting find came to light, in February, 1995. It was in the form of a cast iron, and very heavy, plaque, bearing the royal Arms of Charles II and dated 1660. The latin inscription was barely legible but assumed to be *Dieu Et Mon Droit.*

The cast iron plaque bearing the coat of arms of Charles II.

The plaque was donated to the Town by Mr Hugh Wagstaffe and Mrs Diana Cocker, the children of Mrs Doris Wagstaffe who died last year. Mrs Wagstaffe's husband, Lawrence, died in 1948 and was a well known solicitor in Barnsley, with offices at No 16, Regent street from 1925 to his death.

The plaque had previously rested in the cellar of the Regent Street offices, until on the death of Mr Wagstaffe, it was removed by the family to Gawber Road, where they lived at that time and then to Limesway,

Gawber where Mrs Wagstaffe finally lived.

The supposition in the family was that the old plaque had adorned the old Court House in Barnsley and I think it can be safely assumed, from the following facts, that this conjecture had a certain amount of truth in it. Firstly, at the time of the Commissioners Act of 1822, for the Lighting, Paving, Cleansing, Watching and Improving the Town of Barnsley, John Whitworth was appointed the official architect responsible for laying out the roads and buildings within 1200 yards from the late Moot Hall, which had been pulled down two years earlier. He marked the boundary of the Moot Hall with large stones and I believe he was responsible for moving the plaque to the cellar of his offices which at that time, or later, were, by coincidence, also at No 16 Regent Street. The plaque must have lain there for over one hundred years until it was removed, fortunately for safe keeping, by the Wagstaffe family.

The plaque had obviously been cast to commemorate the restoration of Charles II to the Throne; but I also feel confident in speculating that it was at the time of the opening of the new Moot Hall, built about that time, to replace an earlier structure which had fallen into complete disrepair. This was also to facilitate the resumption of the 'Sessions' in Barnsley which had been discontinued due to the state of the old building.

The plaque is now at Cannon Hall awaiting restoration; I was told by Mr John Hislop, Barnsley Conservation Officer, that a small quantity of paint still existed on the surface of it.

Now to other Relics: a Toll Bell, a Wall Clock, and the Larger Clock in the tower.

There was also a fine portrait of Sir Gervais Cutler, of Stainborough which had hung in the Court room. It was known to be at the Cock Inn in Shambles Street as late as 1870, but nothing is known as to its present whereabouts. Another vanished relic - No further comment.

The Moot Hall Bell

Inscribed 'T. Hilton, 1786' Erroneously recorded by early historians as:- 'T. Hylton Wath 1786'.

The Bell Foundry at Wath-upon-Dearne is known to have existed from 1613 to 1808 being situated in Smithy Lane (now West Street) and run by the Hilton family for two centuries. Thomas, who cast the Moot Hall Bell was there from 1774 to 1808, but alas, it was said, 'Poor Hilton! his foundry operations never enriched him; but many a tuneable bell in Yorkshire Steeples bears his name'. The village used to be up to see the metal run into the mould when 'Hilton cast a Bonny Bell'.

The Bell was first installed in the Moot Hall after it was cast in 1786 where it then tolled for the market and other purposes until the Hall was

The broken hanger.

The Toll Bell at Cannon Hall.

Beevor Bridge, Hoyle Mill.

demolished when it was sold. During the following 150 years it travelled
and was used in varied places, commencing with its first purchaser Mr
James Porter of Park House, Ardsley. The Porters were eminent colliery
owners in the area and were believed to be the first employers of William
Locke, father of the famous railway engineer, Joseph Locke, as suggested
by an entry in Baine's West Riding Directory for 1822, under the heading
of 'Coal Masters and Merchants' read 'Porter and Co. Union Colliery:
Agent William Locke'. Mr Porter had the Bell removed to his coal staith at
Beevor Bridge, Hoyle Mill, where it was used to announce the approach
and departure of his coal trains - what a come down from its municipal
duties on Market Hill!

However, in 1838 it was to serve yet another cause in the tower of the
new church of St. Paul at Monk Bretton where, for nearly forty years, it
faithfully called the devout of Monk Bretton to
prayer and worship. By 1876 the church,
although not old, had fallen into a sad state of
dilapidation and was almost roofless. It had been
described by the Authority as 'a neat church' but
fell far short of the present standard of even
village church architecture'. It was also
described by some as 'a barn looking structure
and its tower as even less imposing in
appearance than an ordinary third rate factory
chimney'. The materials of wood and stone
appeared to have been, from the first, of the
vilest possible description and thirty to forty
years seemed long enough to allow it to stand.
So, it was demolished and replaced by a new
church. The new church had been donated a set
of six new bells by Miss Bright of Monk Bretton
in memory of her two departed sisters, so the old
Bell was once more 'made redundant', a now
familiar ring!

St Paul's Church, Monk Bretton.

Now that the Bell was no longer needed, the Churchwardens, including
Thomas Marsden, three times Mayor of Barnsley, presented it to Mr G W
Atkinson, the Town Accountant of Barnsley, in recognition of his services
to the church which saw its sanctuary in his office where it remained until
1882, in a silent state. It was early in that year that Dr Van Cauwenburgh,
Roman Catholic priest, called on Mr Atkinson and seeing the Bell in his
office tried to borrow or beg it for use on Holy Rood Church.

Mr Atkinson told the Reverend Doctor that although the bell was his, he
intended to restore it to its original owner, the Town of Barnsley. However,

Canon Crooke and Dr Van Cawenberghe.

after much pressure, and as the Bell and its wooden frame, were very much
in his way, he consented to let him have the use of it until such time as he
wanted it, at a nominal rent of sixpence a year. This was agreed and an
agreement was drawn up, dated 5 April, 1882, by Mr Reginald Bury,

Solicitor, and Clerk to the School Board. In the agreement Dr Cauwenburgh pledged himself and his successors, to pay Mr Atkinson or his heirs, the value of the Bell, £100, should it not be handed back to its owners, on request, three months notice to be given by either party, when the tenancy expired. Mr Atkinson told the Reverend Doctor that although he would take the rent, he would return it to him as a gift for his school funds. At the end of the first year Dr Cauwenburgh punctually paid the sixpence rent, which was, as promised, returned to him for the school funds. Strange to say, this was the only money to have been paid for rent because the following year, in lieu of money, he brought back from Belgium, where he had been to visit his Mother, a box of fine cigars which Mr Atkinson accepted as payment of the rent for many years to come. The Bell was then installed on Holy Rood church, by Mr Edward Flemming, Builder of Eastgate and a member of Holy Rood congregation, where it called all good catholics to prayer and worship and reminded all bad ones of their duty. Here the old Bell remained, although the old Holy Rood church was to become the school hall when a new church was built early this century, until about 1970 when it was removed, prior to demolition of the school to make way for a new road. It was then taken to Cannon Hall where it was put on show to the public. Two years later the Markets Superintendent, at a meeting of the Amenity Services Committee, on 6 June, 1972, reported on the historic Moot Hall Bell, now at Cannon Hall and requested that it might be used in the tower of the new market hall. It was resolved, subject to availability and suitability, that it should be transferred from Cannon Hall and installed in the office tower block of the new retail markets. It was later discovered that the hangers on the Bell were broken and therefore it would be dangerous to use it in this state so it remained at Cannon Hall where it, once more, remained silent.

At a meeting of the Barnsley Corporation Finance Committee, held on 19 December, 1889, a letter was read from Mr Atkinson, offering to give to the Corporation, the Bell and Clock (I shall describe the Clock shortly), formerly belonging to the old Moot Hall and Mr Alderman Blackburn moved and Mr Councillor Tinker seconded, it was unanimously resolved that Mr Atkinson's gifts be gratefully accepted. This was later reported in the *Barnsley Chronicle*, with the hope that the 'Relics may be carefully preserved and jealously guarded for many years to come'.

An interesting development occurred in 1892 when, but for the agreement between Mr Atkinson and Dr Cauwenburgh and 'a box of fine cigars', the Bell might have had quite a different resting place for the past 100 years.

In consequence of Mr Atkinson's gift of the Relics to the Town, a letter was sent by Henry Horsefield, Town Clerk of Barnsley, on 7 July, 1892, on official notepaper, bearing the Barnsley Town Crest, to Dr Cauwenburgh, as follows:

Town Clerk's Office,
Barnsley,
7 July, 1892.

Dear Sir,

I am directed to ask when it will be convenient to you for me, on behalf of the Corporation, to cause to be removed from Holy Rood Church, the bell which was given by Mr Atkinson to the Corporation?

The bell is required for the new Weigh House in the Market Place.

I am, Rev. Sir,
Yours faithfully,
Hy. HORSEFIELD
The Rev. T. Van Cauwenburgh, D.D., Holy Rood House,
Nelson Street, Barnsley.

Dr Cauwenburgh, on receipt of the letter, was surprised and certainly not amused so he replied in a most determined manner to the effect that he was the tennant of the Bell having, in his opinion, paid for its use with the box of cigars for some ninety years to come. The Bell could have remained on Holy Rood Church Hall until as late as 1984, if so required. At a meeting of the Estates Committee on 2 November, 1965, a letter was read from Canon O'Flaherty asking the Council's approbation to present the Bell to Cannon Hall - this was accepted.

The Hilton Bell from near Roche Abbey.

While I was on the trail of the Moot Hall Bell, which at one point appeared to have vanished from Cannon Hall, but fortunately turned up, having been removed to another Department, I came across various other bells of interest, two of which, perhaps, deserve a mention:

The first one came to my notice when I was in conversation with a friend and the subject of bells cropped up. He informed me that he had a large interesting bell at home and invited me to inspect it and I was quite surprised to find a very good example of a Hilton Bell c.1777 which had come from a farm near to Roche Abbey some years ago. It too must have had quite an interesting life but that is another relic, another story and another's research.

The other bell, although of a plain quality, proved to be of great local

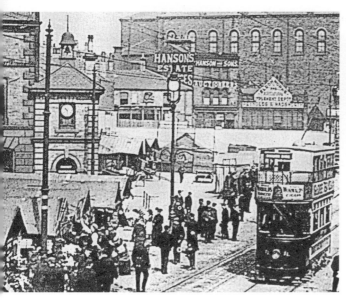

The Weigh House, May Day Green, early this century and the old Weigh House Bell.

interest and I first found it in the Markets office in Barnsley where it had rested for a number of years. After many enquiries I found that it was the original bell used in the Weigh House in May Day Green which was demolished in the late 1930s. It then continued to be used as the market toll bell having been installed in part of what was, at one time, Barraclough's Foundry in the Gas Nook. About 1972 the old market was replaced by a new market hall complete with offices where the bell remains at rest and this bell would probably not have existed if Dr Cauwenburgh had relinquished the Moot Hall Bell in 1892, which the Corporation would have liked for the Weigh House, being built at that time.

The Wall Clock - Tobias (Toby) Fletcher

The clock was the other Moot Hall relic offered by Mr Atkinson, as a gift, to the Council at its meeting on 19 December, 1889, and which was gratefully accepted. It was also agreed that a plate be inserted in the clock stating whence it came, and how it came into the possession of the Corporation; this was carried out and the plate was inscribed 'This clock which formerly hung in the old Moot Hall in Barnsley (pulled down in 1820) was given by G W Atkinson, Borough Accountant Barnsley, to the Barnsley Corporation in January 1890'.

Tobias (Toby) Fletcher, who made the clock for the Moot Hall, was a member of a famous local family of clockmakers and he lived from 1750

Moot Hall wall clock at Cannon Hall

to 1811. His premises were quite a small brick building situated where Royal Street now stands, next to the White Bear Hotel (Royal Hotel since 1835). He was quite a character and a man of facetious bent whose famous saying 'quietness is best', come about, as portrayed by John Burland in his 'Annals of Barnsley', when he got his posterior well roasted on the fire at the King's Head Hotel at the bottom of Market Hill. In his usual jovial mood, he was making fun of John Helme, a member of the 21st Light Dragoons, who had limped in, having been kicked by his horse but Toby went too far and John, loosing his temper, held him on the fire back until Toby cried 'So Quietness is Best'. His saying became quite proverbial in the town and local people often used it when they got into argument.

The clock was a half-case hanging clock with a large circular dial and the movement, although having only one weight, was so constructed as to strike at each hour and the name on the dial, as that of the maker, was Tobias Fletcher.

Mr Atkinson, for many years, had often heard Mr Edward Calvert, linen manufacturer of Crow Well Hill, Sheffield Road, speak very highly of an old clock which hung in his linen warehouse and which always kept correct time. Mr Calvert was originally the Traveller, then the Partner and finally the Successor of Mr John Cordeux. Mr Atkinson, being the son of a clock and watch maker and having something of a mania for clocks, became very interested in what he had heard so he went to see the old clock at the linen warehouse on Crow Well Hill. He found it hanging on the wall and covered with lint which had accumulated over the years and all that Mr Calvert knew, at that time, was that it was hanging in that position when he first entered the warehouse many years before. By now Mr Atkinson's curiosity was increasing and so he asked Mr Calvert to ask Mr Cordeux what he knew of the clock's history and later, in the presence of others, Mr Calvert said that he had learnt from Mr Cordeux that the old clock had formerly hung in the old Moot Hall and that his father had bought it when he was a boy, in the early years of the present century. He had the clock removed to his warehouse, where it has ever since hung, a period of fully sixty years. After hearing this account of the clock he told Mr Calvert that, if ever it had to be sold, he would like to buy it. Eventually Mr Calvert died and the business passed to his younger brother, Mr Miles Calvert. When, later, Mr Cordeux was negotiating with Mr Calvert for the sale of the premises on Crow Well Hill and all the furniture and fittings, including the very clock, he remembered Mr Atkinson often expressing his wish to buy it and waived in favour of him, his right to buy it. So, at last, Mr Atkinson, in November 1871, finally purchased the clock from Mr Cordeux and at the same time asked him if it had really hung in the old Moot Hall. He assured Mr Atkinson that it had hung there and that it was removed from that old building to his father's warehouse where it had ever since hung.

Now that he had finally got possession of the clock, he decided to have it thoroughly renovated, as far as was possible and firstly he requested Mr Benjamin Gaunt, a local watch and clock maker, to remove the clock to his premises for the repairs that were needed including repainting of the dial. When this was done Mr Burrows, cabinet maker, repaired the case and Mr Henry Goodyear painted the case black, relieved with a gold moulding. By then, in all its glory, it graced the wall of Mr Atkinson's office for a number of years, but, unfortunately, like the bell, it was large and ultimately felt to occupy too much space.

The answer came in February 1878 when the Mechanics Institute moved from the Central Chambers in Church Street, (now the site of the Technical College) to the rooms provided for it in the Public Hall Buildings. The committee had no clock to put in the reading room so Mr Atkinson informed them that they could have free use of the clock until either, they got one of their own, or until such time as he would require its return. The committee gladly accepted the offer and it was at once removed to the reading room, where it hung for many years. When, later, Mr Atkinson gave the clock to the Corporation, it was still hanging in the reading room and he trusted the Council to allow it to continue to hang there until a reading room, in connection with a Free Library, was established.

An interesting report, in the Civic Review of November 1952, stated that the clock was still on the wall of the reading room in the Public Library and very reliable in its time-keeping. It is now at Cannon Hall together with the Bell where, perhaps, these valuable and interesting relics of Barnsley's past will eventually be, with great pride, shown to the public.

The Tower Clock

After exhaustive enquiries, and many trails with dead ends, the possible existence or whereabouts of this clock are still unknown to me and I would be interested to hear from anybody with any knowledge of it.

However, let us see what is known of its history:-

I have already stated that we know Edmund Rogers, in 1646, left a bequest of £10 'for erecting of a clocke in the Towne Hall in Barnsley'.

There exists a very mutilated and incomplete account, relating to the clock being installed in the Moothall in 1649 (opposite above).

As this account relates to the pre-1680 edifice, it would be unlikely that the clock was worn out in about thirty years so we can presume that the clock was built into the later Hall. It was installed in a small clock tower above the Hall and it had two dials, the first one facing Church Street. This side could be seen from the Star Inn at the top of Star Lane (where the top part of Regent Street now stands) whereas the other face pointed west and

DISBOURSEMENT FOR THE CLOCK IN THE MOULT HALL.

Monies laid out about the settinge upe of the Clocke in the Moult
Hall, August, Anno Domini, 1649.

	s.	d.
Imp. to Symon Stones that brought yᵉ clocke, sett it upe, and stayde with it four daies and four nights	vij	—
For Richard Shearwood for nayles	iij	—
„ Robert Denton for nayles	—	viij
„ Boards and other timber	iij	—
„ Lead to the plumm̃er	v	x
„ Eight pound of ironn	j	iiij
„ The wrights for theire worke	xx	—
„ Drinke to them	ij	—
„ Binds and Crooks	—	vj
„ Gudgings and plats	—	xij
„ Other two peniworth of nayles	—	ij
„ A locke for yᵉ clocke doore	—	iiij

Fragment of an account relating to the installation of the Tower Clock.

could be seen from the market stalls. Under this side of the Hall stood the
Pillory and the stocks.

It was said that the clock was often out of repair and some of the local
lads used to climb the building and turn the hands as they pleased. Its
condition is well recounted in a poem by Robert McLintock who also
refers to the state of the 'Mute Hall', which obviously was when it was at
its worst, before demolition.

ON BARNSLEY TOWN CLOCK
Barnsley Town Clock is often wrong;
It tells many lies with its hands and its tongue.
But you know it is old- perhaps in its youth,
It was more accustomed to speaking the truth.

I'm well informed its nurse takes great care,
To make it go right and its faults to repair;
But tho' he has failed in many cases,
He says it could do with a pair of new faces.

Some of its faults, permit me to mention:
Perhaps by mistake, perhaps by intention,
It often does speak when it ought to be dumb;
One would think it was drunk with brandy or rum.

At times it goes fast, at times it goes slow;
At times it does stop, and one step will not go,
A learned friend of the faculty saith,-
For want of pulsation, and shortness of breath.

The house where it dwells may suit mice and rats,
Or it may accommodates owlets and cats:
In its windows and walls there are many breaches,
It may be a haunt for fairies and witches.

It is called the Mut Hall, I think it is mute,
That suitable name I will not dispute;
For no human voice is heard in the place:
It's a nuisance to man - to the town a disgrace.

The following account from the eighteenth century churchwarden's records are interesting and, together with others, bear out the regular repair and maintenance required. Note that the account was not settled for seven months after it was issued.

The amount of fifteen shillings per annum for winding the clock remained the same on accounts dated from 1740 to 1756, inflation being quite unknown in those days!

When the Moot Hall was demolished, the clock was purchased, at the same time as the bell, by Mr James Porter who took it to his residence at Park House, Ardsley. After talks with Mr Douglas Redfern, whose family

Park House, Ardsley

lived at Park House for many years, until recently, Miss M Mosby who has researched the history of Ardsley and Gordon Devenport who lived in the vicinity of Park House when he was young, it seems there was a possibility

The Dovecote at Park House, Ardsley.

that the clock had been installed in a Dovecote on one of the old outbuildings by the House.

The outbuildings were demolished some years ago to make way for modern shop units and no positive knowledge of the clock or its whereabouts has come to light. Maybe somewhere, sometime, somebody will find the answer.

So much for the description and travels of the Moot Hall relics as my research, which was carried out with enormous pleasure and satisfaction, has brought to light.

STOCKS, PILLORIES AND PRISONS

A short sharp shock as a punishment for anti-social behaviour is not an invention of the present day, in fact it has been approved by honest citizens as far back as one thousand years ago when stocks were first illustrated in Anglo-Saxon manuscripts.

Before describing our own stocks let us take a look at some of the early statutes relating to the use and establishment of this form of punishment.

Although we know the stocks existed in Anglo-Saxon times, we are uncertain of the actual date of their introduction, however, in the Second Statute of Labourers, 25 Edward III 1350, provision was made for applying the stocks to unruly artificers and in 1376 the Commons prayed Edward III that stocks should be provided in every village.

In 6 Henry IV 1405 an Act was finally passed stating that stocks must be provided and placed in the market place of every town and village. If local authorities failed to do this they could forfeit their right to hold market and that, in those days, would have been a most serious matter for any community.

Another Act passed by Henry VII decreed that vagabonds and idle persons were to be secured in the stocks for 'there to remayne by the space of three dayes and three nights without food except bread and water and then driven out of town'.

Another Statute of James I decreed that any person drunk and convicted shall be fined five shillings to be paid within one week, and if not, shall be committed to the stocks for a period of six hours.

The stocks were a form of punishment for blasphemy, drunkenness, breaking the sabbath, poaching and various other offences of a minor nature. They certainly held their occupiers to public ridicule, in fact it was the public participation which ensured the success of them; perhaps a revival at the present time would not be a bad idea!

The Constable, by way of Common Law, could put offenders in the stocks to secure them, but not by way of punishment. The more important duty of the stocks was to deter men from crime and I feel sure that they would have this very effect but the general use of stocks lapsed towards the mid-nineteenth century.

Stocks were constructed in a fairly common way, two stone pillars grooved on the inside to hold the wooden planks which had the holes cut out to accommodate the legs of the prisoners, as in the illustrations of the Silkstone stocks. They usually had a seat in the form of a plank of wood or stone slabs, not too comfortable, of course.

Towns and villages were often also equipped with a pillory which was similar in some ways to the stocks its main difference being that it was constructed to hold the prisoner's arms and neck whilst in a standing position. Not many still survive but two good examples can be seen at Coleshill, Warwickshire. The pillory was abolished in England in 1815 except for the serious offence of perjury but was finally discarded in 1837.

Near to the stocks and pillory often stood the whipping post, or in some cases, like the one at Silkstone, one of the stone pillars of the stocks was used for this purpose. It was also very common for the convicted person to be tied to the back of a cart and whipped round the streets, for all to see. It was a punishment often imposed on women and vagrants as well as for other offences and as late as 1740 prostitutes were whipped through the streets of London. On the local scene, John Bedford was charged at Barnsley Sessions in 1770 with entering Royston Church and stealing Communion Plate for which act he was sentenced to be publicly whipped in three market towns on their market days.

Material evidence of the Barnsley stocks or pillory no longer exists but fortunately, as illustrated, we still have the stocks at Silkstone which were restored in 1978/79 with their original stone pillars, the larger one being

The Silkstone Stocks.

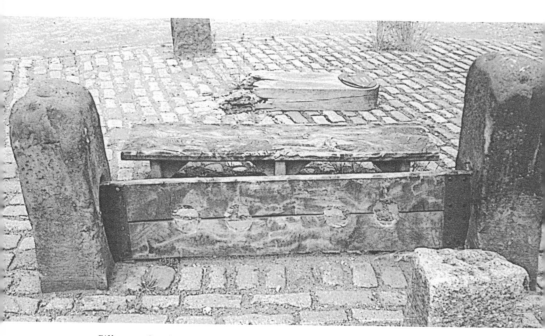

Silkstone Stocks, a commendable restoration and maintenance is ongoing

also the whipping post, and in their original position on Stocks Hill.

It is pleasing to see this restoration, especially as Barnsley was, at one time, an ancient parochial chapelry of Silkstone.

Although no material evidence of the Barnsley stocks exists many records of the site and use of these pieces of municipal furniture are in evidence in the Record Offices. Both the pillory and stocks were sited on the west side of the Moot Hall by the market, the pillory being a little higher up (under the clock) than the stocks which were opposite where the Midland Bank now stands, and where at that time stood two shops.

The pillory was last used about the year 1780 but the stocks were in use much later, as we shall see. The seat section of the stocks, on which the prisoners sat, remained in position but the stocks themselves were kept in the Cock Inn yard in Shambles Street, when not in use and it is most probable that they were constructed all of timber for ease of portability. After the Moot Hall was demolished in 1820 they were placed in any convenient part of the Market Hill but by 1824 they were in a very dilapidated condition and for the next twenty years were considered to be a thing of the past.

However, by 1844, the Commissioners of the Town were determined to have them replaced and a set of new stocks were ordered to be made. These were made by a local joiner whose account book stated '8 October, 1844, To Magistrates, Barnsley, Stocks £5-15s'. They were made to run on wheels for easy storage when not in use and the very next day, 9 October, 1844, for the first time in twenty years, stocks were used in Barnsley for two men, William Yates and Thomas Foster, and for quite trivial offences, the usual punishment being four hours. For about the next sixteen years they were often in use but when, in 1868, Superintendent Sykes became the new Superintendent of Police, it was considered they must have been destroyed before that time. However, it was also said that the stocks were last seen on the south-west corner of the old police drill yard, in the region of our present Town Hall, and that they were broken up in the year 1871 to be used for firewood.

This pillory is to be seen at Mdina, Malta

Finally, a couple of anecdotes, perhaps worthy of mention:-

It was recorded that in 1716 drunken men broke into the Old Chapel on Back Road (now Eastgate) late one night and took away the pulpit. It was found the next morning by the Watchmen (police) placed upon the stocks on Market Hill.

In the courts of Barnsley on 15 April, 1433, Henry VI - Inquisition by Oath of John Whetley - The jurors say that the township of Notton have repaired their stocks as in the penalty of Xs assessed upon them, therefore, they are exonerated.

And in conclusion, an observation regarding punishment in the thirteenth century in Barnsley, to which one must draw their own thoughts:-

By an early Charter under Ecclesiastical Rule at the time of Henry III - At the instance of Monks and bears date at Clarendon 6th February 1249 - "Monks claimed Right of having Gallows".

Prisons and the Barnsley 'Grates'

Imprisonment, as a punishment, had evolved and was well established by the reign of Henry VII. Freedom could usually be bought, consequently it would have been unusual to have found many of the wealthy class locked up.

Up to the early part of the nineteenth century prisons were not regarded as primarily for punishment or, indeed, for the protection of society against criminals. Many offences were punishable by death or transportation which was, obviously, protection and punishment enough. In fact, at that time the number of offences to which capital punishment was applied had reached more than two hundred.

Although the main use of prisons was to hold prisoners awaiting trial or sentence, or for debtors until their debts were paid, an exception was the Houses of Correction which were established to cope with vagrancy. After the suppression of the monasteries and their alms-giving function, the Elizabethan poor laws decreed that able-bodied vagrants were not entitled to poor relief. The Houses of Correction were not just to punish, but to reform vagrants, rogues and sturdy beggars by hard labour and other ordeals.

The very earliest prisons were usually in castles or large houses but later on many parishes had temporary lock-ups called cages often situated on the village green which were used for the temporary custody of prisoners before their conveyance to a more secure prison.

In 1877 prison administration was transferred from the Counties to the Home Office where it still remains.

The old prisons in Barnsley were known as the 'Grates' and the earliest one, of any significance, was situated below the Moot Hall, as I have mentioned in a previous chapter. Its origin was probably as old as the Hall itself but the following early extracts from the Churchwarden's accounts are quite interesting:-

Richard Oxley, Churchwarden in 1622, noted in his accounts -
LAIDE DOWN TO PETER ROBINSON FOR HIS
ATTENDANCE ABOUT THE GRAITE AND FOR GETTING
STAPLES AND NAYLES MADE FOR THE SAME — 7d
Edward Oxley, in 1632 -
MONEY LAYDE DOWN FOR HIS CONSTUBBLESHIP -
PAYDE FOR KEEPINGE SOWDEN BOY IN GRATE WITH
MEAT AND DRINKE SEVEN DAYS — 1s6d
In 1633 -
PAIDE FOR TWO BOARDS AND NAYLES FOR MENDINGS
OF THE GRATE 11d.
PART TWO B

Old people said it got its name from a large grated or iron-barred window, through which prisoners could talk to their friends and receive food and drink. It was not unknown for friends to take ale late at night when they would pass a long straw through the grate to enable prisoners to enjoy a good drink! The heavy door was made of black oak studded with iron nails and was situated opposite the east side of Market Hill above the present position of the Arcade. After the Moot Hall was demolished in 1820 the door was moved to the premises of George Goodyear, carpenter, in Jumble Lane where on 19 September, 1825, (a very windy day) it fell onto John Widdop and broke his thigh. John was only nine at the time but later became a leading member of the Chartists, was very prominent in literary circles and owned a large collection of books and papers.

In earlier times, people spoke of the fun provided by the Sessions, when prisoners who had been sentenced to flogging could be observed receiving their punishments. They were stripped to the waist, fastened to the back of a cart, then driven slowly round the Moot Hall, once or twice according to the sentence, while being flogged by the Constable.

A bizarre incident of these times occurred for one prisoner, Nell Wagstaff, who found truth took her further than she ever anticipated when on advice from her friends that 'truth went a long way', she pleaded guilty to stealing and was promptly sentenced to seven years transportation.

This old Grate was mentioned in a deed of 11 November, 1809 when James Pattrick, Linen Manufacturer, purchased a dwellinghouse situated in the Market Place, occupied by William Crossland and recently used 'as a gaol'.

In a further deed of 11 July, 1823, Barnsley Commissioners, after the Act of 1822, purchased the dwellinghouse in the Market Place, below a building lately belonging to James Pattrick and 'part used as a prison'.

This dwelling house, the subject of these deeds, was one of those below the Moot Hall where William Crossland, whose wife sold muffins and teacakes, was at one time the market stall-setter, a carpenter by trade with a workshop in George Yard and the gaol was below the house.

After the old Grate became really dilapidated and was no longer in use, sometime before 1809 as assumed from the above mentioned deeds, two more prisons came into use. These were known as the top and low Grates but for a short period before this, a cellar at the corner of the present Royal Street was used to hold prisoners and the Sessions were held in the White Bear (Royal Hotel).

The top Grate was situated in the old overseer's office, which was also used as the Court House until the new Town Hall/Court House was opened on 25 September, 1834. The overseer's office was part of the old workhouse which was built in 1735 on the site of the old Brookhouses' Almhouses in St Mary's Place, where Sadler Gate now stands. The entrance to the prison was under the staircase leading into the courtroom and thought once to have been a store cupboard; it left little room for any prisoners to move. This top Grate was under the care of Frank Batty, Constable and Master of the Workhouse which at that time and for several years, was housed on the opposite side of the street in the premises of

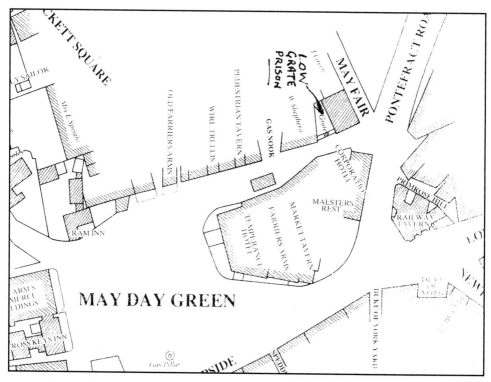

Location of the Low Grate Prison - the building was demolished in 1900.

Parkinson & Creaser, Linen Manufacturers. The low Grate, which was the main town prison, was situated at the top of the Gas Nook near to the end of Pontefract Road and is shown in the plan of May Day Green which was drawn about the year 1850. It was built, according to the date on the head stone, in 1807 and was probably used until some time in the 1840s.

About 1870 the building was seen to be in a very rickety condition and quite unsafe. The old Grate door was still there, with its two keyholes, but had been moved from the centre of the building to the corner and the old Grate was now used as a stable being finally demolished about 1900 for road widening.

The low Grate was well used and prisoners were incarcerated there after the Luddite, Grange Moor and Keresforth Hill riots of 1812, 1820 and 1829 respectively.

The greatest number ever placed in this Grate was in 1829 during the weavers' riots when it included William Ashton and Jim Newton for their part in the firing of Mr Jackson's house on Keresforth Hill, and punishment for this offence was death. A scheme to get them out was devised by a female friend who put a light through a small grate and tried to set fire to the door. The smoke was seen by neighbours who raised Harry Woodcock ,custodian of the Grate and one of the town Constables who although he was about 76 years of age at the time, came quickly and opened the door. Newton dashed off while Ashton held on to the assistant Constable, who had just arrived on the scene thus allowing Newton to escape, even though he knew that his own recapture was inevitable.

To prevent this happening again a square piece was cut out of the inner door and an iron frame inserted having a strong iron door fixed to it so that it could be opened and the inside viewed therefrom. This also served to pass the prisoners' food through.

Another attempt to break in was made at the end of February in the year 1838 when William Denton, alias William Harrison, of Ardsley, was apprehended at Dewsbury and charged with burglary. He was brought to Barnsley and placed in the low Grate but at midnight on the following day, other members of his gang, armed with crowbars and picks, attempted to break open the door. They were foiled in this attempt so they climbed up onto the roof and began to remove the slates where the noise awoke two men in an adjoining house who raised the alarm. The gang decamped and left their tools behind and at the following Courtday, Harrison was brought before the Magistrates and committed for trial.

In 1839 both Grates were used at the time of the Chartist troubles when John Widdop, as representative of the Northern Union, was arrested on 15 August, 1839, and taken before the Magistrates. He was placed in custody, although it is almost certain that it was in the top Grate and not the low

The Police Superintendant's House, built in 1856.

Block of cells to the rear of the Superintendant's house, Westgate.

The West Riding Courthouse built in 1879.

Grate. The next prison to be built in the town was in 1856 when the County and Borough Police Act was passed. It was in this year that Yorkshire formed its new county police force and a new residence was built in Westgate for the new Superintendent of the County Constabulary, Mr Sykes, together with a block of cells at the rear.

In 1879 a new West Riding Courthouse was erected on a plot of land on the corner of Westage and St Mary's Place, next to Superintendent Sykes' house and the new prison cells.

One advantage of the new prison cells was that prisoners could be taken directly from the cells across the yard and into the Courthouse. Previously they had to be taken along St Mary's Place to the old Courts in the Town Hall, where crowds of onlookers would be gathered to enjoy the scene.

In 1901 the old Town Hall was converted into a full-time Police Station and new cells were built between the present building and Sadler Gate. The old workhouse and overseer's office were demolished to facilitate this, together with two very old cells under the Town Hall.

In 1964 the present Police Station, new Cells and Magistrates Courts were erected between Westgate and Churchfields, as part of the new town development plan.

THE MARKET CROSS OF BARNSLEY

No relics of a bygone age have greater interest than ancient crosses. Our ancestors placed them by the wayside, at crossroads, in churchyards and more often in market places. In the middle ages, in England, crosses were frequently set up in the market places for it was thought a good thing to put even trading under the protection of heaven.

Many are still to be seen, in various conditions although in many cases only remnants remain, partly due to the destructive work of the Puritans in the early seventeenth century. The original cross at Banbury was destroyed in this manner and so were the famous three Saxon crosses at Sandbach in Cheshire, now restored.

Barnsley once had its market cross, which I imagine was, unlike the beautiful examples at Barnard Castle and Salisbury, quite a simple affair. The nearest existing example we have is situated at Monk Bretton, (though this was not a market cross as such), it has been moved slightly in recent years to allow larger vehicles to negotiate the road round it.

WHERE was the Barnsley market cross situated? Many have asked. I will try to answer this question, with the help of past local historians, parish registers and ancient deeds.

I found the earliest evidence of the existence of a market cross in Barnsley, at the time of Edward I, in an old deed. This ancient deed, dated

The Cross at Monk Bretton

about the year 1280, stated that Alexander Portbref, of an old Barnsley family, granted to Thomas, son of Robert Del Rodis, a messuage in the town of Barnsley, lying near the way called Westgate, inter alias. The interesting point was that one of the witnesses to this deed was Hugo ad Crucen de Barnsley, or translated, Hugh at Cross of Barnsley. This Hugh was alive on 26 November, 1299, and was one of the jury at York in a case relating to the Prioress of Nun Appleton and Lady of Manor of Worsborough.

The last positive recorded siting of the cross was in February 1719 by John Warburton who was the son of Benjamin Warburton of Bury, Lancashire, and being a rather eccentric character he was buried, in 1759, in two coffins, one of oak and one of lead, due to his fear of worms and wriggling creatures. However when he died he left a prolific quantity of topographical manuscripts, maps and his journals, which now form part of the Landsdowne Collection in the British Library. In 1718/19 he embarked upon two tours of Yorkshire to carry out surveys for his maps of Yorkshire and his second tour commencing at Bedale ended in 'Black Barnsley' in February 1719. While in Barnsley he recorded the size of the market place and mentioned 'the cross on Kirkgate'.

Eli Hoyle, a local historian of some repute, wrote in the latter part of the last century, that he had been requested not to forget Mr George Travis who occupied a shop on the corner of Church Street and Shambles Street the end of which Street was known as part of Market Hill at that time. He said many old people, still living, remembered a small patch of vacant ground on that corner now occupied by a clothiers shop, and that the centre of this piece of ground was probably the site of the old market cross which disappeared sometime before the Enclosure Act was passed in 1777. John Warburton mentioned the cross being in Kirkgate (Church Street) and this small patch of land was partly in Kirkgate and partly in the market place (Market Hill). It was also directly opposite the clock tower of the Moot Hall.

Lodges Almanack stated that in 1654 Bans of Marriage were published in **Barnsley Market Place** on three successive market days. This would be due to a Commonwealth ruling in 1653.

An entry in the parish registers of Cawthorne in 1656 stated that 'The intention of marriage betwixt Robart Woffenden and Susan Horsfall both of the pishe (parish) of Cawthorne weare published three several daies at the **Market Cross at Barnsley** and married July the 27th 1656'.

From these two records, one being 'Banns in Barnsley Market Place' in 1654 and the other one 'Banns at the Market Cross at Barnsley' in 1656, it must be assumed that the Market Cross was in the Market Place.

In conclusion, this evidence, together with the positive siting in Kirkgate by Warburton, must surely place the position of the Market Cross on that square of land since it is the only piece of land situated both in Kirkgate and the Market Place.

Probable site of the Market Cross - the junction of Church Street and Market Hill

Part Three

THE 'TITHE BARN' - WESTGATE

Chaucer, reflecting on the size of tithe barns, wrote:
'An officere out for to ryde- To seen hir graunges and hir
bernes wide'

Many very large and picturesque tithe barns still exist, after five hundred and more years and a fine example at Tisbury in Wiltshire was built as sturdily as a parish church, with stone buttresses. The Abbotsbury barn in Dorset is over three hundred feet long but magnificent examples can also be seen in Gloucester, Glastonbury and, of course, locally, at Gunthwaite.

Barnsley, not long ago, had its own tithe barn which stood in Westgate for over five hundred years. What happened to it? One might indeed ask. First some facts about tithe barns in general and their ancient use.

The importance of tithe barns, which were generally built and administered by the monasteries, is demonstrated in their very size and structure, which raised them above ordinary farm buildings. Their main purpose, in mediaeval times, was to store the tithes, pending their use or

The Tithe Barn at Westgate.

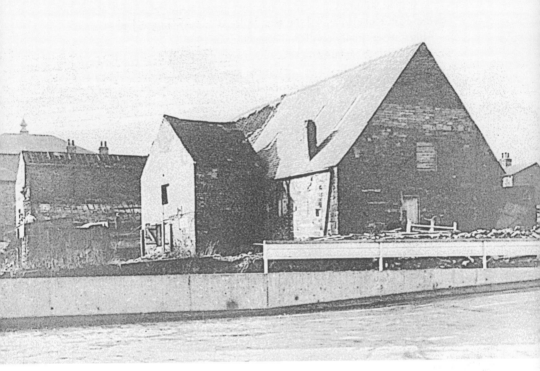

The barn viewed from the rear.

sale. Tithes usually consisted of corn and wool, the chief produce, but could also comprise smaller produce such as flax, apples, cherries, cheeses and honey. A room was usually provided in the barn for the use of the monk or bailiff in charge.

The ancient system of tithes was established and laid down in law by the church, and later, the crown, its purpose being to assist in the upkeep of the local church and Rector. Where the Rector appointed a Vicar to be in charge of the parish, the tithes were divided between the Rector and the Vicar and an Act was passed in 1391 obliging the Rector to use some of the tithe income to support the poor of the parish.

Tithes were calculated at the rate of one tenth of any income from produce and income from labour on the land but allowing an exception for labour on barren, waste, or glebe land.

This system of tithes, in its earliest form, continued until the passing of the Tithe Commutation Act in 1836, under which tithes could be commuted to a rent charge and Commissioners were appointed to agree land values with the landowners. Maps were then drawn up showing the various land holdings, on which the rent charges were calculated and many of these tithe maps can still be seen in local archive and record offices.

Tithes were finally abolished altogether in 1936.

Now, of all the vanishing relics I am writing about, the old tithe barn on Westgate must be the most deplorable and greatest loss that Barnsley has sustained, of its few remaining historical buildings. When one sees what now stands on the site of the tithe barn, a Crown building that after only twenty or so years is costing a fortune to restore, it is not only my own opinion, but that of many others, a virtual 'blot on the landscape'.

Built on the site of the barn, John Rideal House

In December 1967 at a meeting of the Estates Committee, the Town Clerk reported on correspondence with the Ministry of Housing and Local Government regarding the Council's proposal to dismantle the tithe barn with a view to its re-erection on a suitable site. He reported the Ministry's request for an indication as to where and when the barn was likely to be re-erected, if dismantled. The Town Clerk and Borough Engineer also reported on agreed proposals for the erection of a Crown building on the site of the tithe barn.

It was recommended that the Ministry be informed that the Council had no immediate plans for the re-erection of the barn.

Dismantling in 1968, view from Westgate.

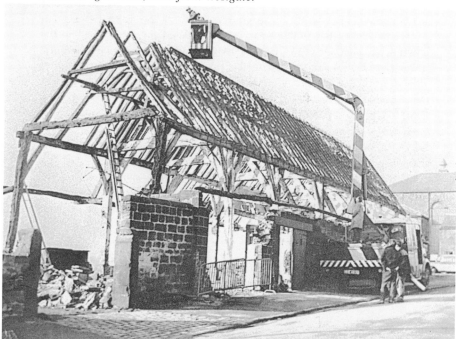

The fifteenth century timbers being dismantled in 1968.

The Director of Cannon Hall was asked to make further enquiries as to the removal and re-erection of the barn, and, the Borough Engineer was asked to arrange for the barn to be dismantled at the appropriate time and the timbers stored. At a later meeting of the Parks, Cemeteries and Allotments Committee it was recommended that the Parks Department should take into storage the structure of the tithe barn, with a view to it's possible re-erection in Locke Park for some suitable purpose in the future. (It would have made a fine folk or farm museum).

So, in March 1968, after more than five hundred years, and still in sound condition, the old barn was sadly dismantled, timber by timber, each piece being meticulously numbered, photographed and drawings prepared. It was then removed for storage in Locke Park until the time of its re-erection.

During the dismantling it was noted that no metal trusses or nails, of any kind, had been used during its construction and all the timbers had been held together with dowel rods or pegs. The aisle posts, resting on their stone stylobates, were made of solid oak and had survived well after the many years. The barn would have originally had a very heavy stone roof but was later replaced in slate and the stone in the walls would have also been altered later.

By 5 November, 1968 (a significant date), after only eight months at Locke Park, the Borough Engineer reported on the theft from their storage accommodation of timbers from the former tithe barn.

In 1977 a report was prepared for the South Yorkshire Archeological Service by Mr Stanley Jones.

He reported on the various types of timber, which then rested in Locke Park, but brought to light a disturbing fact that, from photographic evidence, the total complement of timbers had been greatly reduced since its arrival at the Park. He also noted damage to critical joints in the dismantling stage which 'squares oddly with the professed intention on the part of the local authority to re-erect the building elsewhere in the district'. He mentioned that the details recorded by the Royal Commission on Historical Monuments at No 65 Low Petergate in York were remarkably like those of the aisled barn in Barnsley. This also applied to buildings in Micklegate, York. He then referred to *The Development of Carpentry 1200-1700*, An Essex Study by Cecil Hewitt, in which he writes of aspects of joints and their development and demise. One of the joints which agreed in all detail with that employed in the Barnsley barn, in the arcade/roof plates, was drawn by Hewitt who dated it between 1200-1235. He also

Gary Slater pointing to some of the stylobates from the Tithe Barn at Locke Park, 1993.

stated that other relatives to this particular joint are put at no later a date than 1350. It is possible that certain earlier carpentry features were used in the barn, but it is probable that its origins are no later than the early fifteenth century.

By and during 1984, almost all of the remaining timbers vanished. It was said that they were sawn up and stolen, although I find it hard to believe that those oak aisle posts were easily sawn at all. Some people blamed the miners' strike, others said the timbers were put on the municipal bonfire in the park. I don't know what really happened although I am sure somebody does, and it seems certain that the security arrangements and concern for such important piles of timber must have been pretty abysmal.

As to it's use over the centuries, we know that the original purpose, after being built by the Monks of Pontefract, was to house the tithes of the people of the Manor of Barnsley.

Old map showing the showing the buildings surrounding the barn.

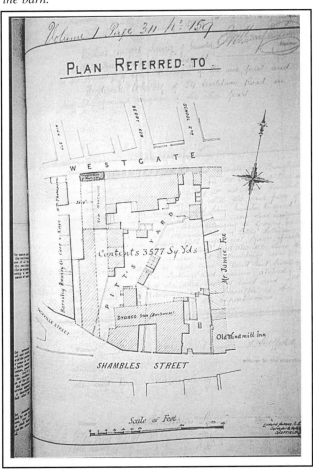

After the civil war and the suppression of the monasteries by Henry VIII, all tithes were made payable to the Crown. Many were allocated to the noblemen of England, but Barnsley remained under the jurisdiction of the Crown and a collector was appointed. One of the early collectors was a man called Edmund Rogers; a highly respected man who held the post during the period 1625 to 1649 who became very wealthy and left many legacies including, as mentioned in an earlier chapter, ten pounds for a clock for the Moot Hall. As a collector, he held possession of the lease of the tithe barn and bequeathed this to the husband of his niece.

During the reign of William III, the Crown granted the Manor of Barnsley, together with the tithes, to William Bentinck, Earl of Portland, who passed it to his son. It remained in the family until 1735 when it was purchased by the Duke of Leeds, Thomas Osbourne.

In 1777, when the Barnsley Enclosure Act was passed, the Duke relinquished his right to the tithes of the Manor of Barnsley in exchange for an allotment of land, together with rent of £182-2-6d, an amount calculated on the area of Ancient Inclosures.

The history of the Westgate tithe barn is closely tied with others which formed part of a complex of buildings situated between Westgate and Shambles Street. The building on the Shambles Street side, we later knew as the Stores Inn, but the other buildings to the rear comprised of a maltkiln and barns called, at one time, the 'tithe barns'; our casualty of 1968, being their only survivor. The house, which formed part of the Inn, was possibly built and inhabited by the Armitage family, from whom sprang the Baronets of Kirklees and the Wentworths of Woolley Park. They were also related to the Keresforth Armitages, a descendant of which family Edward Armitage died in 1673 and was buried in St John the Evangelist's Chapel in St Mary's Church. His tombstone, with the family arms, was in the church until 1820 and Sir Samuel Armitage, born in Barnsley, spent his early years in this house.

The second Sir Gervaise Cutler was a very extravagant man and wasted the family fortune away but soon after he died in 1704, Henry Cutler, the next representative of the family, left his Feudal Hall at Stainborough and brought his family to live in this very house, later to be known as 'Cutler House' where he lived until his death on 20 February, 1725. Egerton Cutler was the next owner of the house, buildings and barns; but being a sailor he died on the coast of Africa in 1742. The family experienced further difficulties in 1754 and sold the whole site and buildings to Thomas Taylor, Mercer, of Barnsley for the sum of £800, although they continued to live there for some years to come. Thomas Taylor was a relative of the Micklethwait of Ardsley where he built Park House and in which he resided for some years helping to raise money in 1735 to build a

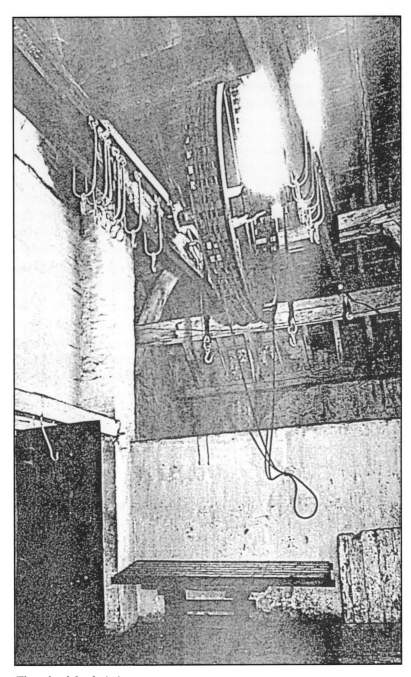

The wheel for hoisting carcasses.

workhouse in Barnsley.

In 1777 a James Hindle lived in the house and George Pitt occupied the Maltkiln, barn and buildings. Pitt purchased the house and land with all the buildings and barn for £1000 and lived there until he died in c1863.

In 1868, the whole site was purchased by William Peckett, a linen manufacturer, who had also lived on the site from 1830; his house was later rebuilt and became part of the Stores Inn, which opened as a beerhouse about 1870. Peckett purchased it from John Wall and Richard Inns who were the Devisees of George Pitt and at that time the barn was used partly as a joiner's shop and partly as a stable.

In 1893, Thomas Berry & Co Ltd purchased the Stores Inn, land, cottages, barn, gighouses, etc. as on a plan drawn on the 1868 Indenture. By 1924 Berrys had gone into liquidation and the Company together with properties, including the whole of the Inn and barn site was purchased by Tennant Brothers Ltd, of the Exchange Brewery, Sheffield.

Four years later, in 1928, the brewery split the site and sold, 2 cottages, warehouse, stables, stores, workshop and slaughterhouse (barn) to Charles Ernest Medlam, who formed a retail butcher's shop in part of the barn, as well as using the slaughterhouse, which was registered.

In September of 1993 I had the pleasure of meeting Mr Ernest Medlam, son of Charles Ernest Medlam, and his wife. The conversation was most interesting and many facts came to light with regard to the barn.

The most upsetting time for the family was when the tithe barn was put under compulsory purchase from his father, a well respected local farmer, butcher and businessman, who passed away in 1974.

Mr and Mrs Medlam of Swaithe.

Mr Medlam told of the many trips to London, the Ministry and many other places, as well as spending a small fortune on his quest to get the compulsory purchase order rescinded, but, alas, as in many other cases, he was unsuccessful.

Before leaving the Medlams, I was told a most interesting story of 'the ghost of the wheel', by Mrs Medlam and later confirmed by Mr Medlam's sister, Mrs Edna Coe, another well known local businesslady. The wheel was a huge thing which was used to lift the heavy beasts in the slaughterhouse. It was heard by Mrs Medlam and another lady, whilst they were working, to start turning by itself, and on more than one occasion. When this happened, the ladies checked for the presence of other people in the barn or outside but found nobody was near. They found this quite frightening, but later it was also heard by a Mr Jack Davies who also swore that he had seen something appear before him and would never return to the barn after this. The ghost was said to be that of a Mr Harry Free, a local resident from the past, but this was never confirmed. Perhaps he will, one day, haunt the corridors of John Rideal House!

In conclusion, it is known that three small pieces of timber survived and are stored at Cannon Hall. Perhaps these together with the stylobates at Locke Park, photographs and drawings could possibly form the nucleus of an exhibition to illustrate the tithe barn in Barnsley.

A wooden peg , one of the few pityful relics of the Tithe Barn.

Part Four

THE LOCKE PARK RELICS
JOSEPH LOCKE - RAILWAY ENGINEER

I wonder how many people, on entering Locke Park, pause at Baron Marochetti's statue of Joseph Locke and wonder who this man was and why he was honoured in this way? I think this can be answered in the words of the Provost of Greenock, in 1841 and printed on the title page of 'The Life of Joseph Locke' by Joseph Devey, 1862.

'The name of Locke will be associated with the triumphs of the locomotive and the marvels of the steam revolution for all coming time'.

Many contemporary and modern accounts have been written of this famous railway engineer so I will write only a brief account of his life, before describing the park and its relics, some of which have vanished over the years, including the loss of the Tithe Barn, as recounted in the last chapter.

Joseph Locke was born at Attercliffe Common on 9 August, 1805. When he was five years old he came to Barnsley with his father, William, and lived in a house on Coal Pit Hill at the rear of number 44 Shambles Street. The house is now part of an Estate Agents office but a commemorative

Joseph Locke.

plaque has been placed on the front of the building, indicating its historical association with the Locke family.

He was educated at the local Grammar School, until he was thirteen, when he was sent to Pelaw, Country Durham, to be apprenticed at the local colliery. Whilst there, he began a lifelong friendship with Robert Stephenson, with whom he shared common interests and ambitions but he became unsettled and returned to Barnsley to work as a clerk at Porter's Pit, where his father was Manager.

After two more years, which were wasted, he resumed contact with Robert and, in 1823, left

Barnsley for good to work at the first locomotive works in the world, Robert Stephenson & Co.

Joseph Locke and Robert Stephenson, together with Brunel, became the world's foremost specialists and leading authorities on all aspects of railway engineering and metal structures, although Locke preferred cheaper and fairly maintenance free brick and stone structures.

Both Locke and Stephenson were convinced, and in 1830, prophesied that a railway network would bring great economic advantages to the Country. Joseph was instrumental in the building of our national railway network and with the exception of the Sheffield-Manchester route, via the Woodhead tunnel, all of his inter-city lines are in operation to-day. He also introduced the railway system to other countries and, at the opening of the Paris-Rouen railway in 1843, was decorated with the Cross of the Legion of Honour.

He purchased Honiton Manor in Exeter in 1846 and in 1847 he achieved an early ambition and became a Member of Parliament. In 1857 he was elected President of the Institution of Civil Engineers.

During 1857 he returned to Barnsley, as an eminent visitor, with crowds to greet him subsequently proving to be one of the Town's most prominent benefactors giving, amongst other things, £2,000 for the Catholic schools and laying the foundation stone of the new Catholic school in Dodworth Road on 17 August, 1858. At the height of his achievements, aged 55, he died suddenly when on holiday at the Buccleuch Arms Hotel, Moffat, on 18 September, 1860, and was buried in Kensal Green Cemetery, London, next to his wife's father, John McCreery, the poet. Locke's colleagues wished him to be buried in Westminster Abbey but his widow, Phoebe, refused on the grounds that she would not be able to be buried with him, however, she did agree to a memorial window in the Abbey instead. The window, designed by Clayton and Bell and funded by the Institute of Civil Engineers was placed in the south bay from the left, in the north nave aisle in 1863. During the First World War the window was removed from the Abbey without any apparent reason. Perhaps it was partly due to Locke's criticism of Government railway policy. It was eventually handed to the Barnsley Council in 1952, then to be stored in a very fragile condition, at Cannon Hall to await restoration. It would be pleasing to see it restored and on show to our people, as a reminder of the important contribution that Locke made to us all during the industrial revolution.

Another handsome and tasteful memorial was erected, as a tribute and in gratitude, in front of the Catholic Schools in Dodworth Road being unveiled in October 1862. It was forty feet high in the Gothic style and when the schools were demolished at the turn of the century, the top section of the spire was removed and erected in the Holyrood presbytery

Holyrood Presbytery with the memorial to Joseph Locke. It was struck by lightning.

garden. It remained there until 1963 when it was struck by lightning and completely demolished.

The Institute of Civil Engineers commissioned a large bronze statue by the Italian sculptor, Baron Marochetti, which was placed in Locke Park and inaugurated on 10 January, 1866, by Lord Alfred Padget. The 4th Administration Battalion of the West Riding Volunteers were in attendance and fired several salutes before the statue was unveiled. After the unveiling they presented arms for a general salute and fired rifles in rapid succession, commencing with the front ranks. It must have been a wonderful sight.

In 1879, stone balustrades were placed round the statue and it is now a Grade II listed monument.

In October 1950 the people of Barentin in France decided to honour Locke and in April 1951, after having taken moulds from the Marochetti figure in Locke Park, erected a replica of the statue near the central part of their twenty seven arch viaduct. The viaduct had been built by Locke and it was regarded by them with pride and affection; they even incorporated it in their coat of arms.

The Park

In 1861 Joseph Locke's widow, Phoebe, purchased seventeen acres of land known as High Stile Field, from the Duke of Leeds, at a cost of £1830. She also provided enough money for laying out and enclosing the grounds, then presented it to the Town in memory of her husband, Joseph.

It was opened as a Park on 10 June, 1862, and a medal was cast commemorating the event which could be purchased in white metal for 6d,

Joseph Locke, by sculptor, Baron Marochetti, errected in 1866.

Observation Tower.

Commemorative medallion.

in bronze for 7/6d or in silver, in a neat morocco leather case for 15/-; all obtainable at J.N.O. Huntley, 7 Market Hill. She also carried out certain wishes of her husband that were not in his will and gave £1000 to the Roman Catholic schools and £3000 to the local Grammar School to found ten 'Locke' scholarships. In 1866 a flagstaff was presented by W Thompson of Hull and installed in the Park during April of that year.

On 18 October, 1874, Sarah McCreery, Phoebe's sister, presented a further twenty acres of land to extend the top part of the Park and also erected a magnificent observation tower in memory of her sister who had died on 15 December, 1866, at the same age as Joseph, 55 years.

The tower was opened to the public on 20 October, 1877, and handed over to the local Board of Health on behalf of the Town. It was designed by a Paris trained architect, R Renee Spiers, and built by a local firm, Robinson & Son. It is now a Grade II listed building bearing a marble plaque on the south side of the tower with the following words:-

'In memory of the Donor of the Locke Park, Phoebe, widow of Joseph Locke, M.P. This Tower was erected and twenty acres added to the Park by her sister, Sarah McCreery, A.D. 1877.'

A medallion was also cast to commemorate the event and is now a highly regarded collector's piece.

A beautiful fountain was erected in the Quarry as 'a tribute of gratitude to Miss McCreery by the Working Men of Barnsley' and completed in 1879.

Sadly due to age, the water no longer flows, but every year it is filled with plants to make a very colourful display.

A further piece of land at the back of the Park, which gives access to Keresforth Hall Road, was given by the

Wentworth family making the Park now about forty acres in size.

An old public footpath ran through the Park, commencing at the site of the old High Stile and extending along the east side of the Quarry through to the rear of the Park. In 1879 it was fenced, with metal railings and gates to the various paths crossing it to allow the Park to be closed at night without blocking the old right of way.

High Stile Field got its name from a high stile, reached by mounting several stone steps, which led to the old footpath just described and was located about twelve yards east of the present lodge and gates on Park Road.

The fountain in its original glory.

The Park, with all its relics of Victorian times, is now, sadly, worn with age but there is still a lot of interest to be found there with a little knowledge of its history.

When walking through the Park, perhaps one might give a thought to a little girl called Fanny Barnes; she was nine years old in 1777 when the last races were held on the old Racecommon, as the land was known before the Enclosure Act when it became High Stile Field, then, as we all know, Locke Park. She was helping her Grandmother, Betty Oxley, with her 'goodies' stall at the time and was knocked down on several occasions by the crowd when coming and going to the stall. She remembered all the spice stalls, gypsy tents and contrivances for gambling on the main road, then known as the Doncaster Saltersbrook Turnpike. Fanny died at Worsbrough Common, aged 88 years, on 5 May, 1856. She had fifteen children, fifty six grandchildren and forty four great-grandchildren - not bad for that little girl.

Relics in the Park - The Lion

As you enter through the main gates on Park Road you will meet with, what is probably the most popular relic of the Park, our old friend, the Lion, situated on guard at the entrance to the Quarry.

Many children have sat on and been photographed with him and, although he is the children's favourite he is also well known to the local vandals who, with their warped sense of pleasure, have continually tried to damage or destroy him completely. Not too long ago they almost

Sadly, on object for the vandal.

succeeded but he was very carefully restored and returned to his present position.

I remember some years ago when the Lion was resting at the bottom of the ABC steps at the far end of the Quarry which was generally known as the Valley Gardens but the far end was always know as the Lion's Den. Many thought this was because of the presence of the Lion, but they were quite wrong since it was not until 1937 that the Lion appeared there, long after the location had become known as the Lion's Den. It was during that year that Dillington Hall, on nearby Worsbrough Common was demolished and the Lion which had been on the Hall's

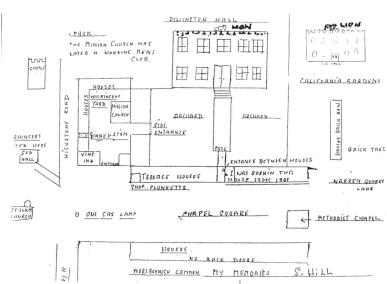

The position of Dillington Hall and the position of the lion in the 1930s.

roof for many years lying passant as in the emblem of Great Britain was preserved and moved to the Park to take up residence in the Den. It was recently moved to its present position for the children once more to admire, and the vandals to wreck.

ABC steps and the 'Meteorite'

The ABC steps are situated at the far end of the Quarry in the Lion's Den where they have been for many years, known to many, twenty six in number and of course, each marked with a letter of the alphabet. Many years ago I climbed the steps to count them and more recently I again climbed then, but this time to reach the path leading to the four Ionic Columns which I will shortly describe.

On the left side, at the bottom of the steps, can be seen a large round rock which many thought was part of the meteorite and even called it 'the stone from outer space'. Once more, they were wrong; it is actually a Silurian boulder from the period of the great ice age and was dug up in the Park a long time ago. It was always a mystery as to how it came to be there in the first place since one would have expected to have seen it at least a hundred miles further north, perhaps near Shap Fell. Locke once built his railway through that area; could it be that he brought it back as a souvenir and it was placed in the Park in later years. Unless somebody knows otherwise, it must remain a mystery.

ABC steps and the 'Stone from outer space'.

Stately columns which once fronted Commercial Buildings.

The Ionic Columns

After leaving the ABC steps the path leads to the four tall stone columns of the Ionic order which were often known as Matthew, Mark, Luke and John and many have stood and speculated as to their origin.

In 1837 it was decided that a new Post Office was needed for the Town and a local architect, Mr W Hindle, was commissioned to draw up plans for a building to be known as the Commercial Buildings. The plans were approved and the building was erected at a cost of £1500 by a Company of Proprietors, in £25 shares. It was situated at the corner of what is now Royal Street, on the site of the old Kings Arms Hotel, previously the Admiral Vernon. The four columns graced the front of the building which was forty feet long and they supported a pediment which formed a portico. The lower room fronting Church Street was used as the main Post Office and Thomas Lister was the Postmaster from 1839 to 1870 who being a well

The Commercial Buildings with the columns removed.

known local personality of considerable literary merit published a volume of his poems under the title of '*The Rustic Wreath*'. He died on 25 March, 1888, and being a Quaker, was buried in the grounds of the Friends Meeting House on Huddersfield Road. The library of the Mechanics Institute was also housed on the ground floor of this building and the Reading and Commercial News room on the upper storey. After 1870 the front of the building was extensively remodelled, making a wider footpath and the columns were purchased in December, 1879, by the Council for £50 and placed in the Park in the position they are seen today.

The Commercial Building was then used by various banks, the Post Office having moved to temporary premises until their own new purpose-built building was completed in Regent Street in 1882. The Town Clerk's office was on the upper floor at the front and Henry Horsfield was Town Clerk from 1879 to 1912 until early in the century the premises were finally demolished to make way for the present bank building.

The Fountain in its early days.

The Drinking Fountain

The old Drinking Fountain is situated near the Park Cafe and almost on the site of the original High Stile although it is very worn and the words on it are fading. Many have quenched their thirst, during the summers of the past, from a little metal cup which was fastened to the Fountain by a metal chain, but not surprisingly, both the cup and chain have vanished.

The Fountain started its life in Peel Square and was formally opened on 29 May, 1859, having been purchased by subscription under the auspices of the Sunday School Band of Hope Union. It was situated on the west side of Peel Square, a few feet from the footpath between Peel Street and Pitt Street. At the opening ceremony, during the usual shower of rain, Mr G. Cooke read a resolution by the Band of Hope Committee as to the necessity of erecting a drinking fountain when it was said that, in the cause of temperance, it was hoped that the Fountain would be successful in slaking the thirst, thus preventing a visit to a public house, many of which were in the vicinity. The Baptist Minister, Rev L B Brown also gave a very interesting address. There was a good attendance at the ceremony, particularly in the juvenile section who, no doubt, were looking forward to taking the waters.

For the next seven years the Fountain helped the cause of temperance but, in 1866, it was reported that the local Board of Health had ordered the immediate removal of the so-called 'nuisance in Peel Square'.

To explain the so-called 'nuisance' one must consider the argument at the meeting of the Board of Health on Tuesday, 9 October, 1866, at which the Committee recommended that the Drinking Fountain in Peel Square should be removed to the Park. One member, Mr Allen, thought 'that it would be foolish expenditure and that a simple cup and chain in the wall of the Park would be of ample provision'.

Mr Battison and Mr Taylor opposed the recommendation and suggested a possible site on Market Hill. The Chairman said Market Hill would be 'the most unlikely site in the Town'. Mr Ostcliffe said that it was 'a great nuisance and just a plaything for the children'. Mr Parkinson was in no doubt that it was of great utility value to the public and he said 'that it was

Theweather worn fountain today.

a reflection on the Town not to have a drinking fountain, like most other nearby Towns, to quench ones thirst and that the Committee should say exactly why they wanted it removed'.

The Chairman stated that the Fountain occupied a large piece of ground and that the Inspector required it for shows etc. for people to stand on. Mr Battison thought 'that it was very ungracious and hoped that the ratepayers would oppose the move, to a man'. He moved that the Minute be not confirmed.

Mr Taylor seconded the resolution.

The members then voted on Mr Battison's resolution with the result that six members voted for and seven against and that the Minute for the removal of the Fountain be confirmed.

At a meeting of the Board on Tuesday, 23 October, 1866, Mr Ostcliffe asked why the Fountain had not yet been removed though it was two weeks since the removal was agreed. He once more said 'that it was a perfect nuisance and asked for it to be removed as soon as possible'.

The Clerk said that they were waiting for the Locke Park Committee to fix a site for the Fountain.

On 26 October, 1866, the Drinking Fountain was finally removed to Locke Park where it remains to this day.

Tanks and guns

One very large and cumbersome relic, which vanished from the Park many years ago, has also faded from the memories of even most of the members of our older generation.

It was the first world war tank presented to Barnsley, by the National War Savings Committee, for its efforts and contributions to the repayment of the short term Victory Loans.

It was a Mark IV Female Tank propelled by a 105 hp Daimler engine to a speed of up to 6 mph, on even ground. Its firepower consisted of five Lewis Guns and its armour has 3/8" steel plating which was both bullet and splinter proof. The Officers in charge were Lieutenants L B Meek and A L Roberts.

This huge war relic arrived at the Midland Station on Thursday 26 June, 1919, when it was driven along Eldon Street to Peel Square to be put under wraps until 1 July (the anniversary of the first day of the Battle of the Somme - a day of special anguish in the military annals of the Riding) there to await its formal presentation to the Town.

On 1 July, 1919, once more it was raining, but a large crowd arrived to join in the ceremony when speeches were made from the top of the Tank by the Mayor, Colonel W E Raley JP, complete in his robes and chain, Sir Joseph Hewitt and other Officials of the Town. After the speeches

The Barnsley Tank.

Lieutenant Meek handed the Tank over to Colonel Fox who then asked the Mayor to formally receive it on behalf of the Town, 'for this generation and generations to come'.

During the previous month, at two meetings of the Parks Committee, it had been decided that the tank, together with a Field Gun, which had also been given with the Tank, should be installed in a suitable position in Locke Park, where it had been publicly stated, that the Tank should stay 'for all time'.

On 19 July, 1919, during the Peace Celebrations, the Tank took its place in the procession, heading for Locke Park, but, unfortunately, it could not keep up the pace, and was left behind in Sheffield Road to continue at its own speed, in easy stages. Rumour spread that the Tank would knock down a wall before it reached its final resting place in the Park and rumour was shortly to be proved correct. The Tank ambled on its way, past the main Park gates on Park Road and on reaching the Kingstone end of the Park,

The Old Canon that once guarded the park entrance.

headed for the boundary wall which, as predicted, crumbled as the Tank poked its nose inside the enclosure. People looking on in awe, witnessed the mighty power they had only heard of and the Tank and Field Gun were then placed on a site where the ground was found suitable to take the enormous weight, after consultations with the Borough Engineer and the officer in charge of the Tank. The site was roughly half way between the ionic columns and the children's playground area and is referred to at a meeting on 22 July, 1920, when the Parks Committee recommended that 'the Borough Engineer be instructed to obtain estimates for fencing round the Tank and Gun in Locke Park'.

As to the final demise of the Tank and Gun, many people I spoke to came up with various vague ideas of the kind: 'I think it rusted away and was buried in the Park' or 'it was scrapped during the last war'. One elderly gentleman who lived near the Park in the 1920s remembered that the Tank was cut up in the Park, by the Blacksmith from Townend. On 5th July, 1926, at a meeting of the Parks Committee, tenders for the purchase of the tank and gun were considered and it was agreed to accept the tender of Mr J. Dunk of Worsbrough, amounting to £31.10.0 (after permission had been obtained from the War Office that the tank would only be sold for scrap). The cutting was carried out by a method using carbide and water and then the pieces were carted away for scrap, by the Blacksmith - regardless of the earlier statement that it should stay in the Park 'for all time'.

The gun's demise was also a bit of mystery but I did talk to a lady, whose cousin said he was working at the Summer Lane Foundry during the last war, where it is claimed the gun was scrapped and melted down for the war effort.

During the 1920s a very old cannon was situated at the front of the Park, mounted on a stone Pedestal and this cannon probably met its end in consequence of a meeting of the Parks Committee on 5 March, 1928 when it was recommended that 'the cannon at the front of Locke Park be removed and the Curator instructed to purchase a vase to take its place on the pedestal'. This large vase was there as recently as two years ago but, need I say it, it was stolen. The only good to come out of this is that it left a prominent place for our old friend, the Lion, who, I am pleased to say, at the time of writing, is still there and in one piece.

The Bandstand

The Bandstand in Locke Park evokes many memories for me; stemming from the late 1940s and 50s, especially the Springtime and those long hot Summers. Some called it the 'Bunny Run' (not to be confused with the Town Bunny Run) when boys and girls paraded round the Bandstand, hoping to meet. Sometimes a band would to be playing and people would sit round enjoying the music on a fine evening.

It now often looks cold and deserted, but the brightly painted colours of the cast iron rails and pillars do endeavour to bring it back to life as merits

Once the central attraction of the park - the Bandstand.

Contracter's name plate - Lion Foundry Co. Limited, Kirkintilloch.

a structure which has achieved the status of a Grade II listed building.

Almost twenty years after the Park was first opened, people were crying out for a bandstand to enhance the Park, but it was another twenty years and more before it finally came about. During the late 1890s, a Park Bandstand Movement had been formed but, alas, this was abandoned on 9 December, 1895.

At last, in the early part of the new century, plans were finally drawn up for a Bandstand, and approved. It was to be 26'3" across and 32'9" high to the top of the weather vane and large enough to accommodate 35 to 40 performers. An estimate was accepted from the Lion Foundry Co. Kirkintilloch and their name can still be seen, cast on the bottom of all the iron pillars.

The final cost came to £326; money well spent!

On Thursday, 11 June, 1908, just forty six years and one day after the opening of the Park, a large crowd of some 25,000 people gathered to see their new Bandstand finally and officially opened - an event which was followed by an excellent programme played by the Barnsley Volunteers Band.

The Paddling Pool

I think the picture of the Paddling Pool, in the 1930s, well reflects the enviable time being enjoyed by the children of that unsophisticated age, poor as it was in many other respects.

Happy summer days in the paddling pool.

The Pool was built of concrete many years ago but it was later filled with sand eventually to vanish under the grass, and although present health regulations would have made it almost impossible to maintain today, it gave immense pleasure to many in its time.

Nearby were the slides and swings, eventually removed due to age but at one time there were also enclosures for peacocks and an aviary nearby. These were last renewed in 1929 but unfortunately in 1966 a heavy storm flooded the aviary and all the birds perished so that in 1967 the last peacock enclosure was removed to make way for an adventure playground which also appears to have vanished. Dare I again mention vandals and their work, which shortens the life of so many of these children's pleasures. Present-day economic circumstances limit the budget for putting back so much that is lost.

The Wishing or Kissing Gate

Of the many old English customs and curiosities, very few individuals will not, at some time, have taken advantage of a wishing or kissing gate.

It was an ordinary gate, but it was hung between a U or V shaped

The Park's romantic gate.

enclosure and there was usually just enough room for one person at a time to either get through it, or become imprisoned. At this stage it was usual to steal a kiss, but it was also supposed to ensure the fulfilment of a wish, if made at that magic moment.

As you will see from the above recent photograph, part of the gate in Locke Park is now missing. It was there in the 1960s but, I wonder, was it stolen or did it just wear out?

I am pleased to say that a restoration will take place in the near future.

The Old Boundary Stone

I was walking in the Park one day when, hidden beneath the undergrowth, I came across an ancient stone boundary marker and could just make out the letters W.D., no doubt representing the old Worsbrough District boundary which went through that part of the Park. Fortunately, although the stone is marked on the old Ordnance Survey maps, it is very well hidden and overgrown, so perhaps it will remain there for many years to come.

To complete the history of the Locke Park relics I would like to make a brief mention of quite an important relic in its own way - i.e. the old toilets adjoining the boundary wall on Park Road which were demolished not too long ago and no doubt will be missed by many a passing motorist. They were very old and could almost have been included in Lucinda Lambton's 'Temples of Convenience'.

Worsbrough District Boundary Stone

Part Five

RELICS IN THE TOWN

The Obelisk - Its Rise and Fall

It all started in 1819 at Folly Hall, situated at the top of Old Mill Lane. It was the residence of William Cooke Mence, better known as 'Lawyer Mence' who held many important positions in the Town as well as practising Law for thirty years and was the son of the Rev John Mence MA, Curate of Barnsley.

At that time most of the area was covered in grass and the road to Wakefield and Pontefract was down Old Mill Lane; the road to Huddersfield was up Victoria Road, then known as Hollowgate, there being no Huddersfield Road at that time, as we know it now, and the way to Sheffield and Doncaster was along Church Street. There was no shortage of travellers at this crossroads, especially those who did not know the way so that both daily and often nightly they would knock on the door of Folly Hall to enquire the way. Lawyer Mence eventually grew tired of giving his 'opinion' as to the way to certain towns and villages, particularly

The site of the Obelisk.

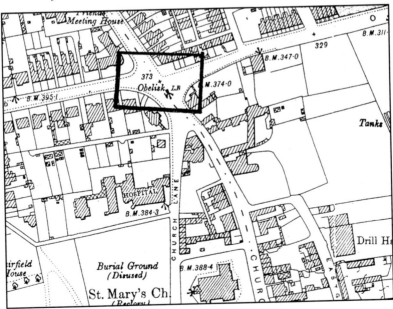

Church Street in the days when the obelisk posed no problem to traffic.

because he did not receive his regulation fee of six shillings and eightpence so decided that the answer was to erect a guidepost for the benefit of all concerned. His motives were twofold, first to give himself a bit of peace and secondly, in a more or less philanthropic manner, to provide a meeting place for weary travellers. To this end, he had a seat built round it and it was thought, but never confirmed that John Whitworth, a prominent local architect, was commissioned to design and build it. It was originally situated on what was Mence's garden, but in later years, part of the garden was taken to widen the road thus, leaving the Obelisk in the centre of the road.

The Obelisk was often known as either 'Mence's Folly' or the 'Peterloo Memorial' since Mr Mence's political views were in direct opposition to those of the persons dispersed at the 'Peterloo Massacre' in 1819, the same time as the building of the Obelisk. When asked by a friend 'what did you build that thing for', he replied, pointing to the date, 'why to commemorate the route of the radical rascals of Manchester!' This was said in jest, of course, but his words got about and so the Obelisk came to be called the

'Peterloo Memorial', inter alia. Although it was originally built as a guidepost, it was later used as a public lamp standard for both gas and electric lamps, a receptacle for a pillar box and even a cab stand, but this was not very popular as it was out of the way.

In 1845 the Obelisk was advertised for sale by the founder's son and a poster was issued stating the conditions of sale. The Commissioners, appointed under the Barnsley Improvement Act of 1822, recognised that, although it stood in the middle of the public road, it was personally owned and they agreed to purchase it for the sum of ten pounds and ten shillings. The Commissioners' resolution stated, on 5 September, 1845, 'that our Treasurer do pay to Mr Mence the sum of ten pounds and ten shillings for purchase of the materials of the Obelisk, the same considered a most suitable situation for the erection of gas lamps and also a safeguard for persons passing along the crossroads, and charge the same to the Lighting and Watching Rate'.

By this time the original lamp on the top of the Obelisk had been replaced by a conical capstone with the lamps fixed on the corners; there was a door on the north side of the column through which the gas lamps were lit whilst the original seating for travellers had proved a nuisance and was removed.

The Obelisk was a fine landmark for Barnsley but its troubles first started in 1868 when Richard Inns, the then occupier of Folly Hall,

Miners Offices in the background.

proposed that the Board of Health either keep it clear of bill posters or remove it.

The Streets and Markets Committee recommended pulling it down but the Board of Health protested and the Committee finally recommended it to be cleaned, repointed, the names of the places to which it pointed repainted and a 'No Bills' notice placed in a prominent position. This was acted upon and so the Obelisk was left alone for a further eight years.

In 1876 Ald Blackburn moved a resolution 'that the Obelisk at the top of Old Mill Lane be removed'. Ald Brady put forward an amendment 'that the Obelisk should remain where it stood'.Once more stories of the Obelisk were bantered in the Council Chamber, but the voting gave ten for the amendment and five for the motion so the Obelisk was saved again.

In 1886, after ten more years had passed, the Parks and Lighting Committee recommended 'that the Obelisk be removed and replaced with a five light Bray Lamp'.

The usual arguments again took place but many of the Town's inhabitants were pleased to see it remain where it was built until 1895.

In 1895, however, controversy, once again raised its head in the Council Chamber and was reported at great length in the Barnsley Chronicle.

The Highways Committee had banned it as an excrescence that had outlived its utility, but this new threat to the Obelisk evoked many new champions.

The *Barnsley Chronicle*, on 23 February, 1895, reported under 'To stand or not to stand', a long discussion which followed the motion, to which Coun E J F Rideal had given notice, 'That the attention of the Streets and Buildings Improvements Committee be called to the advisability of taking down and removing the Obelisk at the top of Old Mill Lane and erecting, it its place, in the most suitable position, a Bray Lamp'.

Ald Wray remarked that it was just a heap of stones but many members wished the old 'relic' to remain.

A letter was received by the Barnsley Chronicle from a Grandson of one of the old Town Commissioners, from Notting Hill, London objecting to its demise.

Another contributor wrote that five months after the corporation had decided to remove it, 'this venerable structure still proudly rears its head to the empyrean'.

So it appeared that the Obelisk had won again.

In 1915 Coun Cretney gave notice of a motion 'To remove the Obelisk on the grounds of obstruction', but later, the motion was withdrawn. It was reported on 18 September, 1915, that the proposal to remove the Obelisk, if persisted in, would have led to an animated discussion at the Council Meeting on Tuesday evening. The withdrawal of the motion however was tactically a wise step.

It is now almost one hundred years since the saga of the Obelisk began, but on to 1931 when it finally ended.

The Fall

The fall started on 10 February, 1931, when the Town Council passed a resolution 'to demolish and remove the Obelisk at the top of Old Mill Lane'.

On 14 July, 1931, after a five month stay of execution, the Town Council rejected a notice of motion to rescind the resolution passed on 10 February to remove the Obelisk. On 18 July, 1931, this was reported by the *Barnsley Chronicle* under the heading of 'oblivion for ostracised obelisk'.

It was a question of sense or sentiment but, alas, one of the ancient landmarks of Barnsley is doomed for destruction, for at the meeting of the Town Council on Tuesday, the utilitarians gained a complete victory over the sentimentalists that the one hundred year old Obelisk at the northern entrance to the town be removed.

In vain did Ald Raley and Coun Rideal extol its virtues and beauty. Soon it would no longer cast its protecting shadows on nervous pedestrians.

Going... going...GONE!

Coun J E Rideal had given notice of motion to retail the Obelisk.

Coun Harold Smith pointed out that the Council had already adhered to the previous decision and confirmed the minutes of the Highways Committee.

Coun Rideal - 'Nevertheless I hope it will remain'.

Ald Cassells - 'Notice of motion is not now in order'.

The Mayor - 'We are bound to continue with this motion in spite of this'.

Ald Cassells - 'Although we have shown we are against it?'

The Mayor - 'Yes'.

Coun Smith - 'Quaint'.

Coun Rideal then remarked that although only two or three voted against it, immediately it got into the Press, protests were made by the whole Town.

Ald Herbert Smith, on a point of order, said that statement was not correct unless Coun Rideal was the whole Town.

The Mayor - 'I think Coun Rideal means his friends'.

Coun Rideal - 'Well the whole Town except No 1 Victoria Road'.

Laughter - No 1 is the Obelisk when you look at it from a distance.

Coun Rideal - 'Traffic can pass on either side; if it goes there will certainly be an accident'.

Coun Smith - 'There has already been an accident there'.

Coun Rideal then went on to speak of her certain beauty and said that people who vote against are not from Barnsley. The Chief Constable was not in favour of its removal and a suitable site for the two lamps could not be found.

Ald Raley said 'It beauty and joy should continue after we are gone' and that it was a great protection for pedestrians. Its removal would accentuate the drop into Old Mill Lane and the only thing to do was to leave it alone.

Ald J S Rose said he had seen it for seventy years, with affection, and suggested that if it was removed it should be preserved in Locke Park or similar place.

Ald Cassells seconded the motion for the destruction of this ancient landmark and it was carried, eighteen votes to five.

Coun Rideal asked that the vote should be recorded.

The Town Council received a letter from W B Wilson of 21, Victoria Road requesting the Council to reconsider its decision regarding demolition of the Obelisk. The Council's reply of 14 July, 1913 stated, with regret, that it was unable to alter its previous decision. Mr Wilson's reply to this was 'the powers that be have, in my opinion, no sense of fitness or proportion'.

Rev Canon H E Hone, who was against its removal, said it gave the Town individual character and also necessitates cautious driving.

'Abject object of official obloquy' - A very apt heading of the *Barnsley Chronicle* of 25 July, 1931, in reporting the fierce controversy of that 'relic' whilst in the throes of its death pangs.

It referred to the almost parallel discussion in the Council Chamber in 1895 and the arguments of that time.

By the 31 July, 1931, the Town was divided into two camps, the pro-obeliskites and the anti-obeliskites. A petition was signed by a number of burgesses protesting against the demolition of the Obelisk, who presented it to the Mayor, Ald Soper. The demolition was postponed and a public meeting convened for 31 August, so that the whole matter could be discussed in full, by all.

Arthur Greenwood, a well known local businessman, summed up the situation in a poem:

THE OBELISK by Arthur Greenwood

Where five roads meet 'tis there to greet
The stranger to the town.
An age worn grey it is this day
And would you pull it down?

One hundred years midst doubt and fears
It proudly holds its head,
In bold relief, its time is brief
Or so the Council said.

Its past is guessed so let it rest
Among the doubts of time;
Its future now depends on how
Our feelings undermine.

A silent mute it does rebuke
The traffic on the road;
It checks their speed, what more we need?
No better sign or code.

Each Barnsleyite will be quite right
if he gathers round,
To defy the risk of the Obelisk
Being raised to the ground.

On 29 August, 1931, the meeting, convened for the 31st was postponed on account of the Feast holiday and pending a visit to the Town by Princess Mary, on 22 September.

On September 24 a start was made on the demolition and on September 25 the Obelisk was razed to the ground. The *Barnsley Chronicle*, on 26 September, reported that residents were amazed that a start had been made on its demolition.

The Obelisk - Going! Pulled Down! Destroyed!

People, all week, stood and discussed that 'Phenomenon' 'Incredible'.

The Rector of Barnsley wrote in Saint Mary's Parish Magazine of the high-handed action of the Council, without consultation with the Burgesses of the Town.

Many objectors wrote that they were not given the opportunity to discuss the matter at a Town Meeting.

Long after, the Obelisk was a topic of conservation - 'This Heap of Stones' 'This Beauty'.

During the construction of the new road layout in 1994, Mr John Hislop recovered a piece of the base of the old Obelisk from 1931.

DRINKING FOUNTAINS AND TROUGHS

In 1885 there were no drinking fountains in the Town, (neither were there any cans of coke or lemonade, to quench the thirst of the inhabitants,) the last fountain having been moved from Peel Square to Locke Park in 1866, as described in a previous chapter.

For a long time before 1885, the need for a supply of pure water for the refreshment of both man and beast, in Barnsley, was in the thoughts of many. Perhaps nobody was more interested in the matter than Mr T F C Vernon Wentworth, who, with a few others, established the Barnsley Band of Mercy. He offered, if a public subscription were commenced for the purpose of erecting a Drinking Fountain with troughs for cattle and dogs, to give £20 or £30 towards it, and, if the enterprise was not quite successful, he would add a further sum to meet it. Unfortunately, in September 1885, and before any steps had been taken for the realisation of his wishes, Mr Wentworth, a man of unostentatious benevolence and kindness to his fellowmen, departed this life.

The Kendray Fountain

Later in 1885, an application was made for a site at the junction of Eldon Street and Kendray Street and this was reported in the Barnsley Chronicle. A response to this was received from Mrs Ann Alderson Lambert (nee Kendray) who now lived in Regents Park London, proposing to be a donor of a drinking fountain, 'for the use of men, cattle and dogs', in memory of her father and mother in whose name the street was named. Her parents

Kendray Fountain, a meeting-up place for the local lads at the turn of the century.

were Francis and Ann Kendray, linen manufacturers, and great benefactors of our Town who had contributed £2000 towards the cost of the Kendray Wing at the Beckett Hospital in 1879 and £4000 towards the cost of the Kendray Fever Hospital, as well as further contributions to these and other causes. Permission for the fountain was gratefully granted and it was supplied by the Metropolitan Drinking Fountain Association in London, erected by Messrs Robinson of Barnsley, at a cost of about £300 and was constructed of Aberdeen Rough Granite.

It was supplied with a drinking cup and chain and it also had a low trough for dogs. The Fountain was inaugurated on 28 March, 1887, by Mr Alderman Thomas Marsden, the Mayor.

During the next forty four years the Fountain gave admirable service to the thirsty of the Town, but, in 1931, with the increasing number of motor vehicles ousting horse-drawn traffic, as with the Obelisk, it was decided to demolish it..

The Mason Fountain

In 1887 it was also proposed that a drinking fountain, with troughs for cattle and dogs, should be placed at the junction of Mount Vernon Road and Sheffield Road.

Many opinions were expressed as to the utility value of this site and the matter might have lapsed but for the generosity of the Rev John Mason and Mrs Mason of Pindar Oaks. Their application for permission 'to erect a Drinking Fountain at the junction of the old and new Sheffield Roads' was

The Mason's Drinking Fountain, at the junction of Sheffield Road, and Mount Vernon Road.

The Mason's Fountain - a survivor to this day - with the inscription 'The Gift of Fanny Mason

granted by the Corporation at a meeting held on 15 December, 1887.

The Corporation also agreed to donate the site and supply the fountain with water from the mains supply.

At a meeting of the Finance Committee held on 27 June, 1888, it was resolved that the completed Fountain should be opened on Coronation day, 28 June, by Mr Alderman Wood, who consented to accept and open it on behalf of the Corporation.

The opposite side is inscribed 'God Save the Queen A.D. 1887'.

It is very gratifying to see that this relic of the past is still in existence on its original site and although the drinking section is not in working order, the troughs are.

The Wentworth Memorial Drinking Fountain

In 1889 the Hon. Secretary of the Barnsley Band of Mercy (Mrs C. Sproat), having a few subscriptions in hand, issued a circular asking for help to erect another drinking fountain as a memorial to the late Mr Wentworth, who, in 1885, had offered to finance a public drinking fountain. Miss Vernon Wentworth was approached with a view to ascertain whether she desired her late father's wishes to be carried out, and with her usual generosity and goodness of heart, she promised a cheque for £25 if the work were taken in hand. Many rebuffs, suggestions and objections to the scheme were received so the project was not successful for a time.

Early in 1895 the Mayor (Mr Alderman Woodcock, JP) promised his

The Wentworth Memorial Fountain which once stood at the junction of Doncaster Road and Sheffield Road.

valuable assistance and as Chairman of the Committee, then formed, authorized the Hon. Secretary to advertise for Plans. In May W Oxley & Sons, Sculptors of Barnsley, were entrusted to carry out the work.

On 12 December, 1895, a handsome gothic structure, over fifteen feet high, composed of Aberdeen and Hill of Fail Granite, was publicly unveiled and presented to the Town by the Deputy-Mayor (Dr Halton, JP) on behalf of the Mayor, who unfortunately was too ill to attend.

This very attractive Wentworth Memorial was eventually taken down during the 1960s, prior to redevelopment and road improvements. I have found no trace or knowledge, whatever, of what happened to its remains - I can only guess!

By the end of 1895 Barnsley now had three first class drinking fountains, with troughs for the relief of dumb creatures, whereas in 1885, ten years earlier, as already stated, there was neither fountain nor trough in the Town.

And so, in the words of Mark Twain - "He took pure, cold, health-giving water - with some other things in it".

The Grade II Listed Dog Kennel

A listed dog kennel in Barnsley? Oh yes, the Town had many interesting and unusual relics, many have vanished, but one that has survived is this listed dog kennel. It must be almost unique.

Its official description reads 'Mounting Block/Dog Kennel, early to mid 19th century. Ashlar stone, small round arched opening with headmould for use as a kennel.'

It is situated at Cockerham Hall on Huddersfield Road, a delightful old building but its use has now changed, sadly, from an elegant private residence to part Chemists and part Solicitor's Office.

The Hall was built by John Taylor, Builder, about 1830. He died about 1833 and it was then sold to an eminent local solicitor at that time, 'Lawyer Mence' of Folly Hall, further down the road.

Folly Hall was then used for the next ten years by his son, Charles T. Mence and in 1851 the law practice was acquired by William H Peacock, the first Town Clerk of Barnsley, who continued there for the following thirty years.

Cockerham Hall was built complete with coach house and stables together with the famous mounting block for the riders, but how many would have thought of a kennel below? Perhaps the builder, John Taylor, was an animal lover and owned dogs.

Unfortunately, Lawyer Mence passed away on 2 February, 1843, having only enjoyed his new residence for about three years but it is interesting to note that amongst the Hall's later occupants was Charles Lingard and his

The Mounting Block at Cockerham Hall also served as a dog kennel.

family, the proprietor of the *Barnsley Chronicle*, which he took over from his father in 1874.

The Kennel, together with the Hall, of course, now has the protection of the laws relating to listed buildings and should be there for many years, for all who pass it by.

George Yard - The Beehive

'You're too interesting a phenomenon to be passed over' Kipling

Have you ever wandered down that quiet bit of old Barnsley called George Yard? At the bottom end is an old linen warehouse with a beehive carved in the stone above the doorway, together with the initials C.R. and the date 1873. Who was C.R. and why a beehive?

The answers can not be found in George Yard; one must go back to 1839 at number thirty three Market Street (now a childrens' clothes shop).

George Yard steadily going to ruin, how long will this old street survive?

Note the the Beehive motive carved above the door.

Joseph Rollinson, a native of Ingbirchworth, came to Barnsley quite early in life and served his apprenticeship to become a tailor. In the early 1830s he married Ellen, the daughter of Mr Tiplady Woodruff, a boot and shoe manufacturer whose place of business was at the top of Market Hill. In 1839, with their three children, they moved into number 33 Market Street and there, in a small way, they commenced business in tailoring and outfitting. In one Directory Joseph was also described as a Clothes Broker.

During the following years, though not active in public life, Joseph and Ellen were very industrious and, with great self denial and conscientiousness, succeeded in building the business up.

In 1856 Joseph decided to expand and purchased numbers 4 and 6 Queen Street (now part of McDonald's). They left Market Street and moved in, Joseph deciding to go into the shoe and boot business while

Detail of the Beehive carving.

Ellen continued in the outfitting side. Joseph purchased his first stock of shoes from Leeds Market which was frequented by wholesale dealers who sold their wares made up into small hampers. This first purchase was made with ready money and the speculation proved to be such a good investment that other purchases were made so that from small beginnings the business gradually expanded.

Now what has all this to do with a beehive? Well, Joseph decided that it was time to have a trade name so he called his shop 'The Beehive', a name that was to become a household name throughout Barnsley and Yorkshire. The business became famous as one of the oldest established boot and shoe businesses in Yorkshire; a virtual 'hive of activity'.

The shop had, in 1838, an earlier claim to fame when it was occupied by William Ask, a watch and clockmaker who in June of that year set up, over the shop, the first illuminated clock ever seen in Barnsley. Such fame did not last very long however since, shortly afterwards, William moved his business to Wakefield and, no doubt, the famous illuminated clock went with him.

In 1863, as prosperity increased, Joseph and his son Charles invested in land on Jordon Hill (Gawber Road) and in 1867 Joseph built a large house at the top of Jordon Hill naming it Bank House. He had handed control of his business to Charles, a little earlier, and now decided to retire and with Ellen, moved into their new residence from where he continued to attend the shop every day, while health permitted, but only in a supervisory capacity.

Bank House is still standing, now as a Guest House, overlooking the top of Hope Street.

In 1872 Charles, who at that time was living with his wife, Mary and three children at number 124 Dodworth Road, decided to further expand, the now very prosperous business, into the manufacturing side of the trade. With this in mind he purchased an old linen warehouse in George Yard from Henry Thomas Fletcher, who had moved there from Old Mill Lane in 1845 to carry on business under various titles, Fletcher & Co., Fletcher Scales & Co. etc.

Bank House on Jordan Hill.

Henry was a member of the well known Barnsley family of clockmakers, being a nephew of Tobias (Toby) Fletcher, who in the eighteenth century had made the wall clock for the Moot Hall.

It is also interesting to note that Henry Fletcher had also built a very handsome villa on Jordan Hill, complete with stables which he named Jordan Villa and which is situated on the opposite side of the road from Bank House, predating the latter by about ten years. This house is also still standing.

Jordan Hill.

Charles Rollinson's next move was to refurbish the old warehouse in George Yard so he had plans drawn of the proposed alterations and these were passed by the local Board of Health. These alterations included the new stone doorway which was adorned by the now famous beehive motif, together with his initials C.R., and the date of opening, 1873, above the showroom window. He was then able to start with the wholesale manufacture of shoes, expanding into boots shortly afterwards.

A section of the George Yard Warehouse today.

The Rollinson grave memorial

A Hive is described as 'a meeting place where workers unite their labour for the benefit of one' - I wonder if this applied to George Yard?

It is sad to relate that about the time Charles opened for business in George Yard, one of his sons, John Temple, died at the age of only five years but worse was to follow when only four years later on 25 October, 1877, Charles, at this early stage in his life and business, passed away in the warehouse in George Yard.

Further grief was to hit the family, two years after Charles died when Joseph died on 9 February, 1879, at the age of seventy, at home in Bank House.

Shortly after the death of Joseph, Ellen let Bank House to Samuel Lindley who had retired as Manager of the Midland Bank and moved to Southport with her other son, John.

In 1888 she sold Bank House and the remaining land at Jordan Hill in 1891/2 whilst continuing to live in Southport until 1892 when they both died in the same year; Ellen on 2nd March at the age of seventy nine and John on 3rd August at the age of fifty eight. Both were brought back to Barnsley to be buried in the family grave at the Barnsley Cemetery where a very fine memorial still stands regardless of the present spate of vandalism there.

The George Yard property was eventually sold in 1896 by Charles' eldest son, also named Charles, who was then living in Australia.

About 1883 the famous 'Beehive Boot Store' in Queen Street was taken over by Joseph Corker who was no stranger to the trade being born about 1840 in Knaresborough, where his family were well known boot and shoe makers, although he had lived most of his life in Barnsley. He was a Freemason and a member of Saint George's Church having started his own wholesale business in Rich Lane off Shambles Street, some years earlier and also owned a shop, in Shambles Street, known as the 'Golden Boot', for about fifteen years. This shop was where Watson's chocolate shop now stands and it is interesting to note that Charles Rollinson ran it for about two years before he died in 1877.

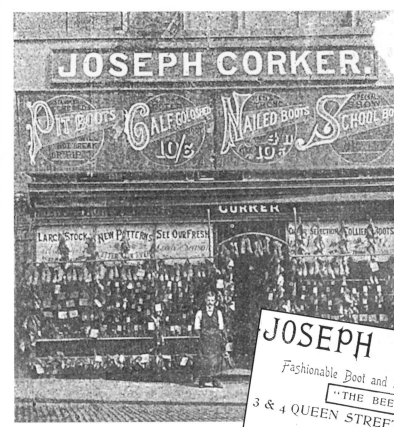

The Famous Beehive Boot Store, the link with the mysterious George Yard Beehive stone carving.

JOSEPH CORKER

Fashionable Boot and Shoe Manufacturer

"THE BEEHIVE"

3 & 4 QUEEN STREET, BARNSLEY

Opposite Peel Square

The Oldest Established Boot and Shoe Business in the County, and always known to sell Good Boots at prices none can beat.

JOSEPH CORKER keeps three times the amount of Stock of Branch Shops and ordinary Dealers, and gives his own practical and personal supervision.

Every description of Boots and Shoes kept in Stock. None Cheaper and none Better. Can fit any feet. Come and judge for yourselves. All Goods warranted. Any not giving good wear will be replaced.

REPAIRS SPECIALLY ATTENDED TO, NO MATTER WHERE BOOTS PURCHASED

HAND-SEWN AND MACHINE-MADE BOOTS AND SHOES SEWED AGAIN THE SAME AS NEW

Joseph Corker

IS ONE OF THE MOST PRACTICAL SHOE MAKERS IN THE TRADE

Corker gave up his wholesale and retail businesses when he took over the Beehive, so that he could give his full time energies to run it.

Joseph Corker proved to be, as the advertisement says, 'one of the most practical shoe makers in the trade', paying special attention to his bespoke department and making sure all his repairs were always promptly executed.

Mr Corker died in 1909 and was laid to rest in the Barnsley Cemetery, after a service at Saint George's Church.

The business at Queen Street then only lasted until the outbreak of war in 1914, when it became a chocolate shop.

The famous Beehive is often talked about today so perhaps when you next wander down George Yard, you will remember some of its history and characters.

George Yard - The Stones

George Yard was named after one of Barnsley's famous hostelries, the George Inn, the entrance to which was in the Yard itself where there was extensive stabling for about fifty horses. The building itself is one of our very few surviving eighteenth century buildings and is located at the top of George Yard.

The Stones I am writing of are to be seen against the wall in the entrance to the Yard and their purpose was to keep the carriage wheels from damaging the wall. I will later relate stories of two other examples of the stones, but first, back to the George Inn.

We know that in 1774, at the time of the Barnsley Races, the Inn was kept by John Nicholson. A Churchwarden's Account records:

John Nicholson at the George in Barnsley

s. d.

Wine 14. 0

Ale   2

April 1776.

The wine being for the communion services but the ale was a perquisite of the Parish Clerk for fetching the wine.

At this time the George Inn was one of the leading post-houses in the Town and many coaches stopped there, including the mail coaches to London, Birmingham and Derby, also the Sheffield and Leeds coach stopped every morning at nine am, the fare being £1. 19s.

On 18 December, 1787, the *Leeds Mercury* printed the following advertisement:

'The George Inn, Barnsley, Yorkshire, TO BE LETT and entered on the 14th January. All the capital and good-accustomed Inn, situate in the centre

Entrance to George Yard with ancient stones to keep cart and carriage well away from the walls.

of the Town, now occupied by Mr John Johnson. The premises have been lately much enlarged and improved are in complete repair and contain numerous well proportioned apartments etc. which have been lately fitted up in the most genteel manner. There is good stabling for nearly fifty horses, a very commodious yard and all convenient offices. For further particulars enquire Mr Joseph Clarke of Barnsley; or Mr Joseph Hawksworth of Burton-upon-Trent, Staffordshire.

The Inn was eventually sold in 1798 by Joseph Hawksworth to the Clarke family who owned adjoining premises and they, in turn, sold it to Frances Day who lived there until 1822.

One further point of interest is that the entrance to George Yard was used as a butter market on market days.

The Bank Top Stones

Another example of these stones can be seen at the side of the road at what was Bank Top, now Mount Vernon.

Bank Top is the site of another of the famous posting-houses of the eighteenth century, known as the Rose and Crown or, sometimes, the Three Tuns. It was famous for its high character and good accommodation and was well known by travellers from all parts. In fact, at one time, it was the only posting-house worthy of the name, between Wakefield and Sheffield.

Bank Top Stones, once positioned against the wall of the posting house.

It was on the old turnpike road which passed through Bank Top, Ward Green and Worsbrough village, a road that was not the envy of heavy and cumbrous vehicles in those days.

The posting-house was kept by John Hammond and such was his reputation that travellers preferred it to all other posting-houses on the road and it was selected by many for their stopping place when wearied with travel. The situation was excellent with walks and plantations in the vicinity, said to form part of the grounds and extending beyond High Stone, forming a quiet rural retreat.

The leading victuallers, at that time, in Barnsley looked at with jealousy at the near monopoly which 'mine host', at Bank Top, enjoyed. It was said that they had done what they could to impair his reputation and obtain a share of the patronage so liberally bestowed upon him.

There was a time when sixteen coaches passed up and down Bank Top Hill every day, including the London-York mails. The Hill was very steep and, at this last part of the journey, the horses were so jaded that fresh horses were often sent down from the Inn to assist them up.

The last occupant of the Rose and Crown was a Mr Kelly, in whose hands prosperity began to wane, to the delight of other Barnsley posting-houses, such as the George, now getting a greater share. In the circumstances Kelly became very embarrassed by his record and eventually his licence was withdrawn; the Inn, as a posting-house, was then closed.

Bank Top, in 1811, came into the possession of the Wentworth family who, partly rebuilt it and the name changed to Mount Vernon.

Protecting stones at Pompeii, 2000 years old.

The Pompeii Stones

On a recent visit to Italy, I was walking amongst the ruins of Pompeii when I noticed, that almost two thousand years ago, the principle of stones to protect the roadside and walls, from the wheels of the chariots and carts, was, even then, in existence.

I found the atmosphere there to be very evocative; one could imagine those chariot wheels racing down the roads, wearing away at the stones - then my thoughts were back in Barnsley in George Yard.

On the corner of the Royal Hotel a bricked up archway can be clearly seen this once led to the stables at the rear of the old coaching house.

The White Bear (now the Royal Hotel)

Whilst on the topic of Bank Top, an interesting incident took place on 14 September, 1835.

The White Bear, as it was known at that time, was another fine posting-house in Barnsley and Sarah Hawksworth was the landlady.

On that particular date Princess Victoria and the Duchess of Kent were passing through Barnsley, on their way from Harewood House. They called at the White Bear for refreshment and fresh horses, which Sarah Hawksworth was delighted to supply; however, crowds formed on Church Street and Market Hill so it would have been too dangerous to change the horses there. The answer, of course, was to take the carriages up to Bank Top and carry out the changeover there.

From that time the White Bear has been known as The Royal Hotel, as it is at this time.

On the photograph, one of the main points of interest is the old arched entrance to the stables at the rear. It is at the bottom left hand corner, now walled in with a window.

RINGS AND THINGS

Since the beginning of time rings, of some kind, have played an important role in our lives. Obviously, the one example of primary importance is the one we wear on our left hand.

However, the examples I am about to illustrate are all relics of old Barnsley, all of which are still in place but no longer in use. Without these and thousands of other kinds, life would have been very difficult indeed.

Bracket for holding a winching pulley. Used to steady carts down hill.

The Fitzwilliam Street Ring

The large metal bracket on the corner of the wall at the top of Fitzwilliam Street is a relic of the days when the Hope Calender Works was situated there. The site covers a very large area having many historic links with our past and William Locke, father of Joseph Locke, once managed Porter's Pit there. On part of it was the famous Hole in the Wall public house frequented by many of our well known local characters, such as Tommy Treddlehoyle frequented the house and one of our eminent local historians of the past, John Hugh Burland, the author of the *Annals of Barnsley*, who was born there on 5 April, 1819. There was never any shortage of trade from both the pit and the Calender Works!

The ring on the wall was not really a ring but a hole in the bracket, in which a pulley wheel was inserted. A rope was secured to the heavily laden carts before they descended the very steep hill down to Summer Lane. The rope was then wound round the pulley wheel which, in turn, assisted in steadying the carts as they, slowly and safely, made their way down Fitzwilliam Street. A simple device, typical of the period.

The Canal Rings

Canals were one of our main methods of transport throughout the time of the industrial revolution and well into this century. The canal barges in this area were the means of expansion of our important coal industry, for without them, the coal could not have reached the rapidly expanding industrial markets of the West Riding.

Iron rings in the B & Q car park were once used to secure barges in the Barnsley Canal Basin not so many years ago.

The old Barnsley Canal Basin and Redfearns Wharf were situated in the area now occupied by B & Q DIY Superstore, down Old Mill Lane. Should you visit the store, park your car in the rear car park, there you can tie your car up to the very rings that were once used to tether barges waiting to take on their cargo from the warehouses on the canal side.

Note the wall on the recent photograph can clearly be seen on the left side of the old picture of the Barnsley Basin.

Street Lamps and Rings

Before lamp-posts were in general use, in the 1820's, many streets in the Town had lamps attached to wires. These wires were fixed to rings, on brackets, which were fixed to the walls

One of the old Market Street wall lamps can be seen in this 1960s photograph. The rings remain to this day (inset).

on either side of the street. After the 1822 Act for lighting and paving the Town, we had about fifty of these lamps in various places and some of the rings can still be seen. Examples can be seen on Eldon Street on the building now occupied by Lancasters.

Another good example can be seen on both the recent photograph taken in Market Street, where the rings can still be seen on the walls, and the older picture showing the lamp in place as it used to be.

After 1820, Barnsley was one of the leading centres in the country for the manufacture of street lamps; indeed Qualter and Smith Bros. on Summer Lane supplied lamp-posts to Barnsley Corporation, Yorkshire Electric Power Company and many other areas such as Bradford and Harrogate; they even supplied parts of London.

The Churchfield Rings

This last example of local rings is, perhaps, the most interesting one because it is associated with our ancient fairs, and in particular, Michaelmas Fair. Until 1751 this fair was held on 29 September after which it was changed to 11 October, the difference of twelve days being due to the alteration of the Gregorian calendar.

In 1777, at the time of the Enclosure Act, the Duke of Leeds held the rights to hold fairs and markets but this was subject to the May Fair being held at the east end of the town and the Michaelmas Fair being held at the west end on Fairfield, now known as Churchfield. These rights and privileges were purchased from the Duke, by Deed, by the Local Board of

The Horse Fair at Churchfields, relics of which may still be found.

One of the rusting ring at Churchfields, once used to secure animals during the Michaelmas Fair.

Health, on 12 June, 1861, for the sum of £2,700, subject to the right of a nine foot wide road to Fairfield House.

The old May Horse Fair was held in May on the site of the old Gas Works and it usually ended by two o'clock in the afternoon. The Michaelmas Fair, on Churchfield, was a much greater affair which originally lasted for four days but this gradually dwindled down to one day which was always the 11 October, was always very busy and would continue until midnight. There would be a large variety of horses, cattle and sheep with Market Gardeners in attendance from miles around in addition to many stalls selling a variety of spices and goods.

The rings (as the example in the above photograph) still exist on the wall at the north side of Churchfield and are thought to have been used to tether the horses at the Fair. It has been said that they were once also used for the bears at the time when bear-bating was practiced; I suspect this is just speculation.

SHOP SIGNS

Two of Barnsley's most prominent and well remembered shop signs give an indication of our past retail history.

The first example I remember always fascinated me as a boy in the 1930s when the giant key and knife and fork were prominently placed on the facade of Reynolds & Wadsworth Limited, Ironmongers, at the bottom of Market Hill.

I often wondered what happened to them but I eventually tracked them down to Cannon Hall where the Curator kindly gave me permission to

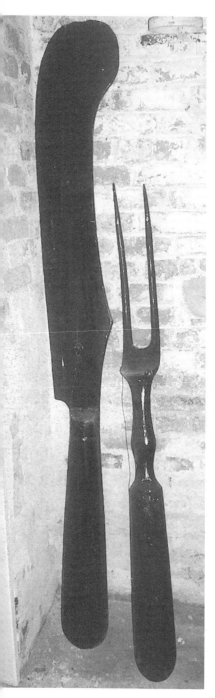

Signs from above Reynolds and Wadsworths.

photograph them. They are quite huge when standing close to them and understandably memories started coming back from fifty years ago.

The recent photographs give an idea of their size and on the old pictures from about 1950 you can see them as they were in situ.

The second example is known to many local

he items in position during the 1960s.

people and also to visitors passing through Townend to Manchester and Cheshire. The sign 'Keep an eye on Townend Stores' with its large painted eye will always be remembered as the Town that kept an eye on you. It will be particularly remembered by myself and my wife,

Townend Stores in the 1970s with the painted eye-sign.

Famous stork sign over Baileys.

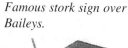

being the last owners of the business before the property was demolished to make way for the Westway Road.

I have previously mentioned that part of the shop front is now stored at Elsecar, for restoration, but, unfortunately the eye has been lost forever.

Any reference to shop signs in Barnsley would not be complete without a word about 'We supply all but the baby'.

This neon-lit sign started life on the very top of No 17 Cheapside, which shop was opened by Edward Bailey, a local Draper, in 1883 where he moved from another shop near the Three Cranes Hotel. In 1968 the business ceased trading and the sign was removed but shortly afterwards another member of the Bailey family opened up at No 5 New Street selling baby linen where the old sign was eventually reinstated and can now be seen by all who pass that way.

THE OLDEST SHOPS

The two timber-framed buildings in this photograph at Church Street probably house the oldest shops in Barnsley.

The right hand building, No 39 has been a Newsagents since the last century. The centre one No 41 has been occupied by our well known Artist, Ashley Jackson, since 1959 and No 43 on the left was also taken by him in 1969.No 41 was very well known during the last war when it housed the local Ministry of Food in 1942.It is interesting to note the timbers protruding from the gable end of No 43 and also the old stone slate roofs.

Numbers 39 to 43 Church Street.

Dow Passage and Sheffield Road once had Boundary Plates - some have been stolen. The example bottom left can be seen in Italy.

FOOTPATH BOUNDARY MARKERS

The particular type of boundary marker I refer to was used a great deal in the early part of this century and one or two examples are, or were, recently still in their original position in Barnsley. Their purpose was, of course, to mark the boundary of the property owner's land and the official line of the footpath.

They were usually made of some hard-wearing metal and the

photograph shows the footpath plate of Denton's Boundary and the other photograph shows the site of Denton's and Mason's shops with their boundary plates still in place. Mason's later became Bennett's Cycle Shop.

There was a good example at the top of Dow Passage on Church Street, showing Rideals Boundary which was recently stolen and a small strip of tarmac now takes its place.

I discovered that these markers are not exclusive to England, I came across an example in Italy which was placed on a very wide footpath in front of a hotel and showed the boundary of the privately owned land.

VICTORIAN IRONWORK

In Victorian times, cast iron was used in the construction of many buildings and structures and when walking through any town or city it is not difficult to spot examples of this type of ironwork, particularly in

The Arcade

Cast iron columns in The Arcade produced by the local foundry Qualter and Hall in 1891.

arcades, as well as lamp-posts and other street furniture.

A good example can be found in Barnsley Arcade by looking at the roof structure but before entering the Arcade, notice the shop on the right hand side, at the Market Hill end. The columns are all made of cast iron, each being marked at the base with the name of the local foundry, Qualter & Hall, also the date, 1891. This particular foundry is still operating and the other well known foundry, Qualter & Smith Bros, although no longer working, was not far away on Summer Lane, already mentioned for its famous lamp-post manufactures.

These illustrations should give you an idea of what to look for and provide incentive for a town-centre walk.

The ' Colossal' Lamp Post

On the subject of ironwork and lamp-posts, it is worth recording a few words about the 'Colossal' lamp-post which stood on May Day Green and is clearly marked as 'Gas Pillar' on this old map from the 1850s. It was erected in 1821 and had the following inscription:-

'This column was presented to the town of Barnsley by Mr John Malam of London, Civil Engineer and Contractor, for Lighting the Town with Gas. A.D. 1821.'

Mr Malam also supervised the building of the new Gas Works. The

Position of the colossal Lamp Post on May Day Green.

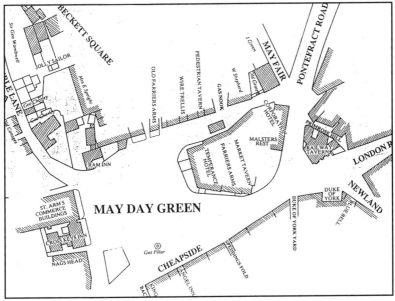

Contractor for the excavation work was a Mr Bower of Dodworth and it was erected on three tiers of four steps. These steps were often used as a meeting place by the Chartists and other organisations.

In 1862 it was discussed by the Local Board of Health and considered to be an obstruction and Mr R Carter suggested it could be moved to Peel Square as the only architectural ornament there was the drinking fountain. Mr Parkinson suggested they could pipe the water into it and convert it into a drinking fountain to replace the present one. However it was finally agreed that it was in the way and on 7 June, of that year, it was removed.

CHIMNEYS

When I recently went out and scoured the Barnsley skyline for any sign of the old factory chimneys I came to the conclusion that Fred Dibnah had beaten me to it. However, I did get a shot of the old Baths chimney with the modern chimney of the General Hospital rearing its ugly head in the background.

The Old Baths opened in June 1874 and is now a listed building being renovated and formed into single person's flats, hence the scaffolding round the chimney which will ensure its place in history long after the new

The old Baths chimney with the General Hospital on the skyline.

Town End and a forest of chimneys at the beginning of the century.

ones have gone. Above is a comparative picture showing just a few of the old mill chimneys at Townend in c.1911. There were literally hundreds of them in the Barnsley area and thousands in the great mill towns of Yorkshire and Lancashire, dating from the time of the industrial revolution. In places like Saltaire near Bradford, magnificent examples can be found, fully restored for many years to come.

Old Bleach Works at Cudworth

I discovered one very nice example out of Town, also listed and in the process of restoration. This one pictured below is at the old bleach works of Henry Jackson & Co, who moved there in the 1850s, from Oakwell, in search of cleaner air for the bleaching process.

It is now getting more and more difficult locating relics of our past but pleasing to know that many things are receiving official listing.

THE PINFOLD AND 'THE LAST POST'

I have known the Pinfold Steps in Shambles Street since I was a boy in the 1930s and have climbed them many times over the years, clinging onto the old central handrail when the steps were icy in the winter and, at the same time, reading the advertisements on the hoardings at the side.

Some years ago, the lower part of the steps was modernised with new railings, but, I was pleased to see that two of the old iron handrail posts had been placed on the footpath at the bottom of the steps. Later I was not surprised to find that one of them was missing so I thought that 'The Last Post' as I called it had better be recorded amongst the relics before that, too, went missing.

Opposite: Pinfold Steps at the turn of the century and below; The Last Post in 1995.

I found it interesting to compare the old with the new:-

The Pinfold was situated on the righthand side of the steps on a level piece of ground near the top.

I can't remember the Pinfold when it was in use but two friends, a few years older than myself, can and fascinated me with their personal recollections of it.

Hector Woffinden, who was in business in Dodworth Road for many years, told me of the times when it was used by the local police for stray animals on Mondays when the cattle market was held on the Kendray market by the bus station. He also told me of the time when one day he and some friends were returning home from St Mary's School and were surprised to find a donkey in the Pinfold, they all had a good laugh - happy days.

Dan Linton, another good friend, told me of the many times he had watched the drovers bringing their cattle and sheep into Barnsley on market days. How useful that Pinfold must have been in those days before motor transport was used for the animals.

The Barnsley Windmill, which was demolished in1845, gave its name to this terrace.

THE BARNSLEY WINDMILL

Barnsley only ever had one windmill which once stood on the north west corner of Churchfield, at that time known as Fairfield. The site retained the name of Windmill Hill long after it was demolished in 1845, but little evidence of its existence remains.

Records show that in 1825, Abraham Pincheon was in possession; an 1828 Directory shows James Cade, Corn Miller, Churchfields, and it is believed the last owners, in 1833, were J & R Gelder. The windmill gave names to Windmill Terrace which stood near to it and also to two of the old Inns in Shambles Street, one being the Old Windmill Hotel and the other being the Windmill Inn. The yard of the latter Inn was a thoroughfare between Shambles Street and Saint Mary's Gate which I often used in the 1940s, before the bulldozers moved in.

The Windmill was said to have occupied high ground above Saint Mary's Church Tower and was quite a conspicuous object as one could well imagine. However it is strange that although it is marked on Thomas Jefferys's map of 1775, which was surveyed about 1767/70, it is not marked on the Barnsley Enclose Award map of 1777, the particular plot having been awarded to Edward Crowther.

It is also marked quite clearly on the large scale Ordnance Survey map of 1850 and it is possible that the survey took place just before it was demolished.

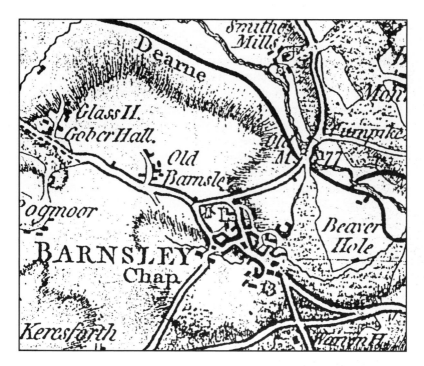

*Above: Thomas Jefferys's Survey of 1775 shows the Windmill as does the
Ordnance Survey Map of 1850 below.*

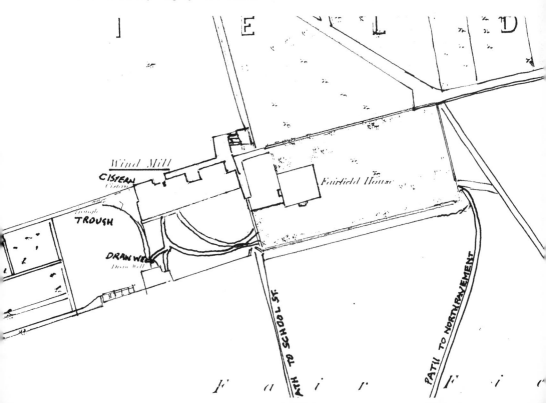

WHAT HAPPENED TO 'ATLAS'?

'Atlas' was well known to many courting couples and cinema goers during the 1930s, 40s and 50s as it was their rendezvous point, at the Alhambra Cinema in Sheffield Road. In the days when queues were commonplace, Atlas would be looking down, keeping a stony eye on things. He was a large carved figure mounted on the corner of the cinema and is believed to date back to the 1920s, when he was carved by Alfie Popplewell, a local mason based in Pitt Street. He was actually cast in pottery clay with a glazed finish.

In 1982 the Alhambra cinema and surrounding area were cleared to make way for the new Alhambra Shopping Centre but fortunately, a businessman, Mr Eric Wilkinson and his wife Elisa, who fell in love with it, rescued Atlas from the demolition men's hammer. They took him home and set him up in their garden at Wakefield, where people have come from

far and wide, on a sentimental journey, to see an old friend.

In 1989 when the new Alhambra Shopping Centre was being built, it was hoped that Atlas would return to Barnsley and used as a centrepiece where couples, once more, could rendezvous at 'Atlas'. It could also have been used as a logo on publicity for the new Centre as well as being a good conversation piece.

Atlas, now a garden ornament at Wakefield, once took the strain at the corner of the Alhambra Theatre.

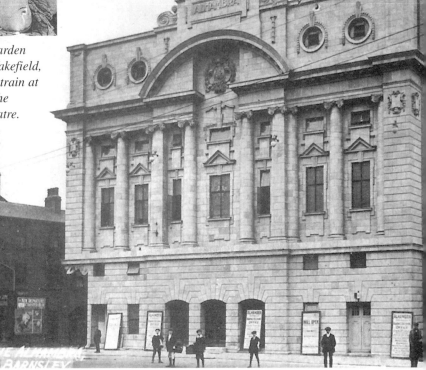

In June 1989 Mr Wilkinson received a letter from the Developers, Greycoat Shopping Centres Plc, declaring their interest in using this, very desirable, centrepiece for their new development. Talks were entered into and architects were sent to measure Atlas and take details. Plans of the new development were then shown to Mr Wilkinson, but, alas, out of the blue, it suddenly appeared that the style would not fit in with the new concept and the idea became lost in time.

'Atlas' still rests in the Wilkinsons' garden at Wakefield but perhaps, one day, he will return to Barnsley to evoke memories of those happy days at the Alhambra Cinema.

BARNSLEY'S OLD GRAVES

It is not my intention to write about people interred in the old graves but to draw attention to the places and periods where the burials took place.

The main Barnsley Cemetery was consecrated on 6 November, 1861 (the Catholic portion 14 September) and the first internment took place on the 1 November, 1861. The place is well worth a visit to see the resting place of the Town's worthies but one grave I will illustrate, particularly its headstone, is known as the Blacksmith's Headstone from 1909, hand cut in York Stone, by an old Barnsley craftsman. Unfortunately, now vandalised.

All other examples of old graves, which I found of particular interest are

Intricate carving depicting the interior of a blacksmith's shop.

now given and all predate the main Barnsley Cemetery and are to be found in chapel grounds or churchyards. For instance there are some forgotten headstones on derelict land off Pitt Street, once the graveyard of St George's Church.

A sad way to remember - two stones off Pitt Street.

Left: Friends Meeting Place on Huddersfield Road contains in its grave-yard and interesting stone dating from 1688 and previously situated at the Quaker burial ground at Monk Bretton. Below: The ground at Huddersfield Road.

There is just one remaining grave in the grounds of what was once Westgate Chapel, now known and used as the Boys Club. It is possible that some of the paving slabs are in fact reversed gravestones.

My final item in my quest for interesting gravestones was to be found at the Club Hedonism (Island Corner Coop). Mr Richard Ledger kindly allowed me to visit the cellars - the site of an old burial ground.

The present-day building stands on the area once occupied by the Methodist New Connexion Chapel, which was built in 1804. In 1872 the Chapel was purchased by the Directors of the Barnsley British Cooperative Society for £700. They used the Chapel building as a warehouse for a

The Club Hedonism and cellars with its intriguing bricked up passage leading to the old Connexion Chapel burial ground.

while before demolishing it and building the present complex, which was opened 14 August, 1886. However, there was one condition that had to be met by the BBCS. Part of the site they had built over was the burial ground and they had agreed to leave an underground passage through the cellar to allow access to the graves. I discovered that the passage had at some point been bricked up, presumably, once the usual period required by law had passed. What lies beyond the end cellar wall?

AIR RAID SHELTERS OF THE SECOND WORLD WAR

Whilst on my travels I realised that, like chimneys and so many other interesting things, the old air raid shelters of the Second World War had just about all disappeared. Upon inquiring after examples my good friend, Hector Woffinden came up with two ones at the rear of 40 Huddersfield Road, a house that was once used by the Auxiliary Fire Service during the war. I remember having a similar type in the back yard of where I once lived. Later I remember, it served as a most useful garage for my Lambretta scooter.

Further along Huddersfield Road and opposite the old Girls High School, is the site of a very early reservoir, built by the old Barnsley Water Company during the last century. The site is know to a few as 'Bailey Hill'

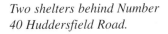
Two shelters behind Number 40 Huddersfield Road.

no doubt because it does give the impression of a motte and Bailey Castle site. I was talking to an elderly gentleman who lived nearby and he told me that the side bankings, which used to house the main pipes, was used as an air raid shelter during the last war.

Site of air raid shelters during and after the last war at Bailey Hill.

Further evidence of shelters from the war years, this time underground type shelters, was unearthed during the building of the new Hospice. They had been constructed under the school playground and served to bring back memories for Mr John Batty, local historian, who was in Standard III at the time of their construction in 1939/40. He wrote an interesting article in the Gawber Church magazine in which he recalled the whole school being lined up in the playground in the same shape as the shelter directly below them. The shelter was about eight feet wide and eight feet high; it seated about 120 people; had four Elson type toilets and was lit by about six paraffin lamps. On at least two occasions it was used by local people during the blitz on Sheffield.

Another pupil at the school during that time, Mr Marcus Studd, had the job every morning of opening the escape hatches to allow fresh air to pass through so that the shelter stayed fresh and dry.

The yard at Gawber School with the Hospice in the background, along with a simple plan of the layout of the shelter.

Above: the site at Park Road and Duke Street where a substantial underground shelter existed until recent times. Some mystery surrounds its purpose, but it likely housed the HQ for the Civil Defence.

Right: Interior of the shelter at Kendray Street as it was during the last war. It was under the Queen's Market and the site was built over so likely it has been filled in.

THE CONVENIENCES OF OLD

The history of toilets has been well covered and illustrated by Lucinda Lambton in her *Temples of Convenience*, however I would like to make two historic observations.

The first is of Sir John Harrington, a godson of Queen Elizabeth I who, it is said, invented the first working toilet that flushed. He installed one in his own house and one in Richmond Palace for the Queen. The first patent was granted many years later in 1775.

The second observation concerns our own Joseph Bramah who, in 1778, perfected and patented the syphonic type of toilet, which was to prove to be the best design for the next ninety-eight years.

Now looking at our own town conveniences: these can be placed into two catagories, one being the full ladies and gents public toilets complete with wash facilities, and the second being the urinals.

In the first category the only true example in Barnsley must be at Peel Square. I would like to acknowledge the help that I received from Mr Steve

'Best sited below ground level' was the view

Robinson of the Cleansing Department, via a lengthy conversation
concerning the social background to
public conveniences and in particular, our local ones.

The Peel Street complex was built
during the early part of this century
when, in Edwardian times, these
matters were not matters to be open-
ly discussed, were matters of mod-
esty, consequently subterranean
places of convenience were constructed regardless of the engineering problems of getting the sewage
away this caused. To this day it is
still pumped up to a tank from
whence it discharges into the main
sewer.

The original glazed earthenware
equipment was made by the well
known firm of J. Duckett & Son Ltd,
of Burnley, who ceased business in
1978. It is still in daily use, after
nearly hundred years, but has recently had a certain amount of restoration, which is scheduled to continue
as funds become available. The original oak doors have been polished
and so has the old copper piping.

Edwardian urinal stalls still serve today

Natural lighting comes from glass bricks set in iron frames positioned in
the roof. I can remember, many years ago, the Salvation Army playing over
the toilets - wonder what the occupants thought? But then, I wonder what
bystanders thought if they caught sight of me entering the place with a
camera!

In the old days it cost one penny (in the slot) to use the toilet and in the
ladies they also had a useful parcel service where the ladies could leave
their items while they did their shopping - the charge was one and a half
pence.

The second category of toilets comes under the heading of 'Urinals',
many of which were built about one hundred years ago in strategic positions around the town. Most of them have disappeared during the develop-
ments which have taken place in recent years. They were intended for the

A vanishing feature of our town - the urinal. The 'Hole in the Wall', Summer Lane.

use of workmen coming home from the pits and other work, especially so after they had called in for a well earned pint. In those days most women stayed at home doing the washing and cooking.

The urinals were often built with the full cooperation of the breweries and the local Corporation. They were often known by amusing names, and a couple are still in use.

There's the 'Hole in the Wall' at Summer Lane, which is situated on railway land and costs the Corporation a peppercorn rent. The example at Park Road, known as 'The Little House on the Prairie' has recently vanished. Then there's 'The Bungalow' at Churchfields, and 'The Cave' at Cutting Edge, both still proving to be a convenience for Barnsley menfolk.

Popularly known as 'The Little House on the Prairie' with lampost and, what appears to be a cable running from the post into the toilet. Since this was taken, 1995, this, yet another relic of the past, has disappeared.

Above: 'The Bungalow'.   Below: 'The Cave' at the Cutting Edge.

To conclude this absorbing subject it would seem fitting to go back to a very early example, not of a public loo, but a private one and partially underground at that. It was recently discovered at Cannon Hall and appears to be mid-Victorian. Some years ago I was studying a map of Cannon Hall when I spotted a path marked that appeared to lead nowhere. It looks as though that path led to the 'unmentionable' - a building constructed for purposes that were considered too indelicate to mark on the plans.

The toilet has a dividing wall in white glazed brick; on each side there is room for a double seat of the 'thunderbox' variety. Below is a sizable tunnel which was probably flushed by water from an underground source. It is pleasing to know that it has been restored with the help of a grant from Barnsley College.

Fully restored to its former glory - the outside loo at Cannon Hall, a credit to those responsible.

Part Six

THE BEST STREET IN BARNSLEY

Pitt Street

When Nikolaus Pevsner carried out his survey of Barnsley, he stated, 'The best street in Barnsley is Pitt Street'. This was mentioned in his well known series, 'The Buildings of England', in which he also noted other buildings of merit including St George's Church by Rickman 1821, Temperance Hall by W Hindle, 1836, Pitt Street Methodist Church, St Catherine's Terrace and St George's Place.

The following picture depicts, indeed, what a typical elegant street of the Victorian period was like. Notice the solid character and neat layout of the buildings, fenced with fine cast-iron railings, together with trees and greenery; the stability of that period is certainly indicated by all of this.

The work of John Whitworth, Architect and Sadler, must be acknowledged, for after the 1822 Act for Lighting, Paving, Cleansing, Watching and Improving the Town of Barnsley, was passed, he was responsible for most of the public buildings and highways in Barnsley. His father was a sadler at the top of Market Hill, and when he died, John

Pitt Street in its heyday - the best street in town.

carried on the business, but also studied at great length to become an architect. He died on 26 January, 1863, aged 83, but, during the previous forty years, he laid out and completed all the turnpike roads in the district, levelled Shambles Street, removed the old Moot Hall from Market Hill, raised the lower end by the Sough Dyke and designed and built the Corn Exchange and the old Town Hall. He planned and laid out Pitt Street, Wellington Street and all the other streets in the area then known as Peashills and he designed no less than forty chapels in or near Barnsley. With William Cooke Mence of Folly Hall, he founded the Wesleyan Sunday School with six hundred scholars and sustained every office in circuit methodism open to the laity.

John Whitworth

Let us now consider some of the buildings in Pitt Street:-

The Wesleyan Chapel

On 1 September, 1845, in the presence of about three thousand persons, the foundation stone was laid by Thomas Cope, Town Commissioner and, later, Chairman of the Local Board of Health.

Until Thursday, 8 October, 1846, when the new Chapel opened, local Methodists had been using the Westgate Chapel, which had been enlarged by John Whitworth. The Sunday School moved from Churchfield in 1858 to use the rooms below the Chapel, and shortly after this, John Whitworth moved to a house next door which proved to be more convenient for his

The Wesleyan Chapel opened in 1846 was demolished in the 1980s.

work. Another house across the road, known as Manse Chambers, was the home of the Nonconformist ministers until 1922, after which it was used as offices, and is now, a dentist's surgery.

In the early 1980s, the roof structure of the Chapel was said to be unsafe and the building was demolished, due to the prohibitive costs and work involved. Perhaps times were more affluent in Victorian days when this and many other fine buildings were erected? The old chapel was replaced by a modern building (pictures below), the design of which must be a matter of personal preference or is, perhaps, governed by present-day economics.

New Pitt Street Chapel

Temperance Hall

Next door to the Wesleyan Chapel is a fine building of the Ionic order, known as the Temperance Hall. It still stands majestically against the modern parts of Pitt Street, having recently been restored for use as offices; far better than demolition. It was originally built by the Order of Oddfellows, to a plan by W J Hindle, another eminent local architect and the foundation stone was laid by G H Smith on 18 July, 1836, the work costing £1,100 which was raised by shares of £1 each.

Unfortunately it did not, for long, serve the purpose for which it was intended, due to the embarrassed financial state of the Society and within a few years was sold by auction to be used as a furniture warehouse. In 1880 it was purchased by the Temperance Society, from

Temperance Hall

which it got its present name whilst some twenty-five years later it was used as a school, and from 1909 to 1928 a Picture House. After the last war it was first used as the Central School of Dancing and from 1952 became Farnsworth's warehouse. Quite a variety of uses, and, maybe, many more to come, but still there to be admired.

The National School (Ellis School)

George Ellis died on 15 April, 1712, and left £6.13.4d for teaching twenty of the poorest children in Barnsley. The Trustees were left to choose the pupils and, eventually, in 1813, a school was built, opposite Temperance Hall, to house the children. A grant of £700 for this purpose, was made by the Trustees of Ellis' Charity (through the exertions of John Whitworth) and local subscriptions added a further £100 making a total of £800. The school was free until 1850 when a charge was made of one penny per child per week, later to be increased to twopence.

The school was demolished in 1963 and the site used in 1967 for the new Y.M.C.A. building.

St George's Place and St Catherine's Terrace

St George's Place was an attractive Georgian Terrace, at the upper end of Pitt Street, opposite St Catherine's Terrace, another very interesting row of houses. St George's Place was once said to have one of the most

St George's Place

St Catherine's Terrace

pleasing facades of any row of houses in Barnsley and many prominent citizens lived on the opposite side of the road, part of which was later used for the Convent of the Sisters of Mercy.

St George's Church

St George's Church in Pitt Street is our latest sad loss to the demolition men's hammer. It was a fine Grade II listed church designed by Thomas Rickman who was famous for the many churches he designed, all in the Gothic style. He lived from 1776 to 1841 and left over 2000 sketches of Gothic buildings, now in the Ashmolean Museum.

The structure, said to have structural faults, appears to have taken great effort to demolish; this was replaced by a brick building on York Street.

The Church was a 'Waterloo' Church, built out of a Parliamentary Grant

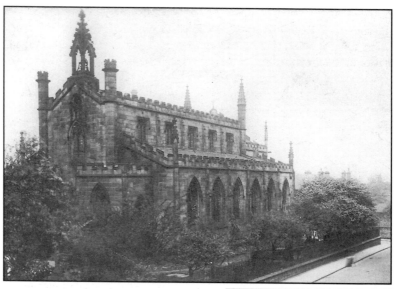

Here endeth another another historical building - a sad day in 1993.

for the building of new churches as a national thanksgiving for the defeat of Napoleon at Waterloo.

The foundation stone was laid, at the south-east corner, by the Grand Master of the Freemasons, on the eve of St George's Day, 1821.

When the Church was demolished, this foundation stone, which contained coins and a brass plate, depicting details of the opening ceremony, was never found. It was thought to have been removed when the new Chancel was built about 1872.

Modern-Day Pitt Street

In 1932, Mr A E Kay, a resident of Scarborough and regular correspondent, wrote the following, being part of a long letter to the Barnsley Chronicle:

"A few months ago I went up Pitt Street and as I looked around, a sob came into my throat - I thought it the most wretched deplorable sight to be found in Barnsley. Why, at the rate of deteriation it will soon be the slum of Barnsley. To think that once Pitt Street was the home of some of our best families; and now, what a disgrace and, at one time, the "main" road to the Park. I suppose New Street will now occupy that position. Well what New Street was once Pitt Street is now. I don't know who's to blame but it is a standing disgrace to some one". *A E KAY*

I conclude this last chapter of *The Vanishing Relics of Barnsley* with the following photograph, of Pitt Street to-day. What would Mr Kay think of it all now, sixty years on?

SOURCES AND BIBLIOGRAPHY

Barnsley Archive Service:

Minutes - Town Commissioners
Photograph Collection
Old Building Control Plans
Pitt St. Chapel-Centenary Book

Barnsley Local Studies Library:

Council Minutes
Obituaries
Almanacks - various
Listed Building List
Old Newspapers
Burial Register
Census returns and Tasker Index

Yorkshire Archaeological Society Record Series
West Riding Registry of Deeds, Wakefield
Widdop, John - Obituary Notice
Tasker, E G - *Barnsley Streets*
Pevsner, Nikolaus - *The Buildings of England: West Riding*
England, W G - *The Growth of Local Government in Barnsley*
Bayford, E G - *Our Markets and Fairs*
Jackson, Rowland - *History of the Town and Township of Barnsley - 1858*
Hoyle, E - *History of Barnsley*
Burland, J H - *Annals of Barnsley, 1744 - 1864*
Wilkinson, J - *Worsborough - Its Historical Associations,1872*. Newspaper Cuttings
Goodchild, John - *Golden Threads*
Hunter, Rev Joseph - *South Yorkshire, Vol 2, 1831*
McLintock, Robert - Miscellaneous Poems
Churchill, W - *History of the English Speaking Peoples*
Devey, Jos - *The Life of Joseph Locke, 1862*
Cartlidge - Rev J E Gordon - *Newbold Astbury & its History-Stocks*

ACKNOWLEDGEMENTS

My grateful thanks to all the people who have helped with information which has assisted me in writing this book and my apologies to any I may have omitted.

John Brailsford (Old Barnsley Plan)
Ruth Vyse, Gillian Nixon and staff at Barnsley Archive Service
Maurice Hepworth - Barnsley Local Studies Library
John Hislop - Conservation Officer, Barnsley MBC
Peter Goodwin - Barnsley Drainage Maps
Johnnie Scott - Barnsley Drainage Foreman (retired)
Harry Brookes - Markets
Brian Murray, Curator, Cannon Hall
Geoff Stoner - Cannon Hall
Paul Gorman, Gary Slater, Derek Walker - Locke Park information
Record Staff - Wakefield Archive Service
John Brailsford - Old map and note - Barnsley
Ian Harley, *Barnsley Chronicle* - Photograph, Peel Street
Keith Wilson, Beevor Court - Assistance at Beevor Hall
Douglas Redfern, Miss M Mosby, Gordon Devenport - Information Park House Ardsley
John Higgs - Information, Cawthorne Parish Register
Stephen Maw - Hilton Bell, Roche Abbey
Neil York - John Cordeux, Rylands' Library
G Crossland, Barnsley Tank
Medlam family - Information, Tithe Barn
Eric and Elsa Wilkinson - Information, Atlas
John Hislop, Geof. Stoner - Moot Hall Plaque
Richard Ledger - *Club Hedonism*, Graves
Hector Woffinden, John Batty, M Laverick - Air Raid Shelters
Steve Robinson, Cleansing - Old Public Conveniences
Dan Linton, Hector Woffinden - The Pinfold
John Batty - Air Raid Shelters

PICTURE CREDITS

INDEX - PLACES

INDEX OF PEOPLE

ASPECTS OF BARNSLEY 1

Discovering Local History

Edited by Brian Elliott

First in the successful series which covers a collection of previously unpublished studies and features relating to the town and surrounding district. This book set the format for the series with its diverse compendium, which relects a varied history of Barnsley, along with the research methods and personal backgrounds of its twelve local authors - some going into print for the first time.

BARNSLEY BOYS CLUB + BLEACHWORK ARCHAEOLOGY
PAPER MILLS + TURNPIKE ERA + RYLANDS GLASS
WATTER JOE + OLD KINGSTONE + A WORSBROUGH HOUSE
HUNSHELF + THORNCLIFFE RIOTS + EBENEZER ELLIOTT
GUNTHWAITE + DODWORTH

ISBN: 1-871647-19-3 256 Pages
108 illustrations £9.95 Paperback

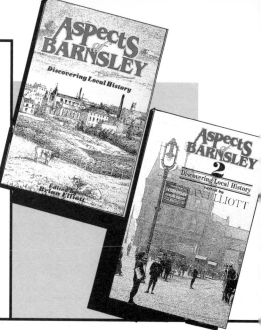

ASPECTS OF BARNSLEY 2

Discovering Local History

Edited by Brian Elliott

Sixteen Local History Accounts

PUBLIC HALL DISASTER OF 1908 + BARNSLEY RACES
LEISURE ACTIVITIES AT OAKWELL 19th CENTURY
EARLY MOTORING IN BARNSLEY
WELSH COMMUNITY IN CARLTON AND SMITHIES
QUACKERY, FIDDLING AND BLOODSUCKING
MAPPLEWELL AND STAINCROSS - 19th CENTURY
NEWSPAPER PUBLISHING IN THE 19th CENTURY
BEGINNINGS OF BANKING IN BARNSLEY + MINING
VERSES
THURGOLAND WIRE MILLS + SILKSTONE RAILWAY
AGNES ROAD SCHOOL in the 40s + CHILDHOOD IN
STAIRFOOT

ISBN: 1-871647-24-X 288 Pages
146 illustrations £9.95 Paperback

ASPECTS OF BARNSLEY 3

Discovering Local History

Edited by Brian Elliott

Seventeen Local History Accounts

CURES AND CURIOSITIES OF OLD BARNSLEY
TOWN END in the 1870s + HANDLOOM WEAVERS
TEACHING HISTORY IN PRIMARY SCHOOLS
IRONSTONE MINING AT TANKERSLEY
THE DEARNE and DOVE CANAL + NEWCOMEN ENGINE
PAWNBROKING IN BARNSLEY + MITCHELL MEMORIAL HALL
CHILDHOOD MEMORIES + GREAT HOUGHTON OLD HALL
BARNSLEY IN THE ROCK 'N' ROLL ERA
PIGOTTS DODWORTH ESTATE + PENISTONE MARKET
E. G. BAYFORD TRIBUTE + DEARNE WATER POWER SITES
WHEN BUFFALO BILL CAME TO BARNSLEY

ISBN: 1-871647-26-6 272 Pages
146 illustrations £9.95 Paperback